Dry-Curing Pork

Dry-Curing Pork

HECTOR
KENT

Make Your Own Salami,
Pancetta, Coppa, Prosciutto,
and More

WARNING: Pregnant women should not consume **any** uncooked dry-cured meats due to the risk of listeria.

Dry-Curing Pork
978-1-58157-243-8

Published by
THE COUNTRYMAN PRESS
P.O. Box 748, Woodstock, VT 05091

Distributed by
W. W. NORTON & COMPANY, INC
500 Fifth Avenue, New York, NY 10110

Printed in
The United States
10 9 8 7 6 5 4 3 2 1

DEDICATION

To DeVeau, whose name should be next to mine on the cover of this book,
and Harlo, who keeps my head in the right place. Love you both.

On your way home from the bookstore, go buy these ingredients:

1. A pound or two of boneless pork loin (at least a foot of it, and the best quality you can find.)

2. Kosher salt.

Now you can make coppiette, on page 52, the first recipe in the book.

CONTENTS

My wife and I were lucky to be raised in families that valued growing or sourcing food locally. After we moved away from these homes, we were always happy to purchase the wares of local growers and producers near our home in Oregon. As teachers, we prioritized the ability to start our summer adventures on the first day of vacation over growing all our own provisions. On one of our shopping trips into Portland to a favorite butcher, we noticed as we purchased a piece of beef that everything in the display case was locally produced, except the salami. This was in the days before Olympic Provisions and Chop Butchery began selling their products, and as we drove home we expressed our surprise that the only available salami, while tasty, was coming from a major producer from over 500 miles away. Even more concerning, we had no idea where the pork had originated.

Our home at the time was on the desert end of the Columbia River Gorge. We looked out on the barges, trains, and windsurfers while enjoying the plentiful sunshine and poison oak that eluded the western half of the state. We spent hundreds of hours roaming the hills above the river walking through the wildflowers, windblown oak groves, and rolling hills of yellow grass that surrounded our home. One day, as we looked around at the blanket of acorns around us, we thought: Why not raise our own pigs? Why not make our own salami?

We continued the conversation, and over the next few months we came to realize that many people were thinking the same thing—including our favorite butchers. But it was our friends down the street, Quin and Dave, who get the credit for getting us started on this dry-cured adventure. Several weeks after mentioning our interest in pork one night over dinner, we returned from an early-summer adventure to discover that they had purchased two piglets for our families to share. The animals were now happily roaming their yard and fattening up on acorns.

Acorn-fed pork is legendary, argued to be the best in the world, so as we cut into our first dry-cured ham, we had thoughts of a delicate prosciutto on the brain. We quickly became aware of the hard, salty reality. Dry-curing is an art and a science, and we knew we needed guidance—the random recipe off the Internet didn't do a pig justice. I turned to the small number of resources responsible for introducing thousands of people to dry-curing—*Charcuterie* by Michael Ruhlman and Brian Polcyn, and *Cooking by Hand* by Paul Bertolli. I read them cover-to-cover, learning everything I could, and we started practicing—just a shoulder now and then. It was a couple years before we took on a whole pig again.

Through this learning process, I assumed I could find the necessary teaching materials to continue progressing. I had started homebrewing a few years earlier, and there were countless books and Internet resources available—not to mention the whole craft-brewing culture springing up around the developments of homebrewers. I assumed things would be similar in the world of dry-curing, but I quickly realized that the same resources didn't exist. While I could find the occasional step-by-step instructions for making a

specific product based in vaguely Italian traditions, there was no consistency. This was adequate at first, but I'm a biology teacher, and I wanted the actual science. I wanted to know which variables I should be paying attention to, and how these variables could be adjusted and manipulated to perfect my final product.

At the same time, like many people who enter the world of dry-curing, I wanted to create authentic Italian dry-cured meats. As I pursued this goal, I realized that imitation of Italian products and methods is a great teaching tool, but imitation doesn't lead to authenticity. Every region of Italy, not to mention every region of the Mediterranean in general, has its own dry-curing style. The magnitude of the diversity was deeply confusing. What I've come to realize is that since people embraced the flavors and conditions of their homes in creating their dry cures, imitation wasn't actually a priority.

There's nothing more authentic than buying a pig from the woman down the street, cutting it up on a folding table in your yard, flavoring it with dried herbs from your garden, and hanging the cuts in your shed. The trick was finding the background knowledge that would allow me to perfect the combination of my ingredients as opposed to copying a technique used on another continent. This search for knowledge introduced me to the research of legendary Spanish meat scientist Fidel Toldra. I realized the information I sought did exist, but it would require a journey into the world of European meat science.

Fast-forward a few years, and the result is what you have in your hands. I've filtered through thousands of pages of research and data on dry-cured meats and pieced together the critical aspects in the pages of this book.

At its core, this is meant to be a book that teaches you so that at some point you won't need it anymore. In it, I present a basic process you can follow step-by-step, but also give you the science behind the process, so you can dry-cure anything, Italian or not. If you don't have access to an Italian butcher, it doesn't matter—you can dry-cure any meat, whether or not it's exactly how the Italians do it. True authenticity will be attained by perfecting the process of bringing together all your own variables, in a way I can't show you, because those variables are unique to your place.

Finally, I never set out for dry-curing to become a major part of our lives. We've now left Oregon for Vermont, and unexpectedly every autumn, as the last leaves fall off the maples, our extended family gathers and we begin the process of paying our respects to the recently killed pigs. We do this not with band saws to cut pork chops destined to become lost in the depths of the freezer, but by carefully segmenting whole pieces of beautifully marbled, dark-red muscles into their natural forms. We continue the ode to pork by salting, drying, and finally thinly slicing meat onto a plate with a little cracked pepper and lemon.

You will find an unexpected and welcome revival of old methods—and I don't mean old methods for our family, because we don't come from a tradition of dry-curing. What started as we walked through the oaks and wildflowers has developed into a celebration of family and food. The grill is hot so we can snack on the bones, a keg of homebrewed fresh-hop beer is on tap, and we know that in a few months we will cut into a coppa that has never traveled more than 500 feet from the grove of trees where the pig spent his days. If I'm lucky, I'll get a taste of the flavors of summertime and home.

CHAPTER ONE

The Art of Dry-Cured Meat

The term *cured meat* primarily refers to meats that have been modified through the application of either salt, sugar, or smoke. Curing can affect the flavor, texture, color, and shelf life of a piece of meat. Most cured meats are cooked, but *dry-cured* meats are a subset of cured meats, which are never cooked and—as the name implies—have been dried, usually by hanging during the cool winter season. Originally developed as a method for preserving meat, the combination of salting-then-drying allows the meat to be stored at room temperature for long periods of time; the meat can be eaten safely without ever being cooked.

Primarily attributed to, and perfected by, the cultures of the Mediterranean region, in actuality dry-curing was and still is practiced worldwide. With the advent of modern refrigeration, dry-curing is no longer necessary in many cultures, and it's the antithesis of the standard supermarket pork, which has been pumped full of water to increase the weight and, therefore, profits. The process survives, however, because it highlights a complex array of flavors that no other meat preparation can. The best dry-cured meats are among the most expensive and sought-after foods in the world, and showcase the perfect marriage of a region's indigenous flavors and environment.

At its heart, dry-curing is based on very simple scientific processes, which prevents the growth of microbes by salting and removing water. The Euro-

peans have turned it into an art form, with masters of the craft honing their skills through hundreds of years of inherited background knowledge. The best dry-curing is built on a foundation of tradition, but this focus has created an air of inaccessibility surrounding what is, at its heart, simple.

This book is designed to remove the mystery from dry-curing. It will teach the basic processes, but will also provide the science behind the traditions and show you how the same four variables—meat, salt, time, and microorganisms—come together to create every type of dry-cured meat, whether it's salami, prosciutto, speck, or pancetta.

This chapter will provide some of the background of how to use these four elements in concert, hopefully providing you with some understanding of the science behind dry-curing.

DRY-CURING VERSUS CURING VERSUS CHARCUTERIE VERSUS SALUMI

We live in a melting pot of cured meat cultures. The confusing terminology surrounding cured foods is a result of the unique mixture of different cultures, traditions, and techniques found in North America. Cured meats are found worldwide, but the vocabulary we use to describe them is primarily European in origin. There is no standardized terminology, and terminology is often mixed up and used incorrectly. It's a mess, in a uniquely American way, and as with much of our food and drink, this mix of cultures provides a foundation of flavors and techniques that we can build on—but because they're not tied to one tradition, we can develop our own regional flavors and specialties.

Here are some of the most common terms associated with cured meats:

Curing, as in *cured meat*, is a very general term and references the changes associated with coating meat or fish in salt or sugar, and/or smoking. These products can be cooked or uncooked. Cured meats are very common in the American diet, and encompass most deli meat, ham, bacon, hot dogs, smoked salmon, many sausages, and every recipe in this book.

Charcuterie is a French term that includes a wide range of cooked and uncooked cured meats, sausages, pâté, and confit. It can also be applied to the recipes in this book. *Charcuterie* has become an accepted term to describe what you might call "artisanal" cured meats, regardless of the country of origin.

Salumi refers to Italian cured meats, both cooked and uncooked. Many types of salumi are dry-cured, but the term also includes cured and cooked items, such as mortadella and cooked ham. There are thousands of different types of salumi, and as soon as you try to find a single defining recipe for anything, you'll realize that every region has its own techniques and recipes—or uses the same name for two very different products. It's confusing, but it can be entertaining and rewarding to dig around and uncover obscure styles of salumi. If you don't speak Italian, you'll quickly start to recognize the flaws of translation when faced with the unique terminology around these products.

Dry-curing is the generic term for meats that have been salted and dried, but never cooked. It's a utilitarian name, which is why you'll see terms *charcuterie* or *salumi* on a menu long before you see *dry-cured pork*, but it's the only term that is specific to uncooked, salted and dried products, and doesn't include things like cooked ham or fresh sausages. As a warning, you'll occasionally see *dry cure* in reference to meats that are coated with a dry rub of salt and spices, but are then cooked—a rack of ribs, or bacon for example.

The Meat

The type and cut of meat determines what product you'll be making in this book, we focus on pork.

In dry-curing, the quality of your final product is directly related to the quality of meat you start with. Indeed, the quality of meat you use is the single most important variable. The best dry-curing in the world, the hams of the Mediterranean, are simply a combination of meat and salt—and they showcase some of the world's finest pork.

Once you have the routine of dry-curing established, put all your energy and resources into sourcing your meat. Until you reach that point, do everything you can to avoid using generic supermarket pork, as the raising and eating of any livestock has a negative environmental impact. Find out where your meat comes from, ask questions about the animal's living conditions and diet, and set a high standard for yourself—if not for the ethical and environmental reasons, then because of the flavor difference. You'll pay a premium for high-quality, local meat, but a dry-cured shoulder will provide you with weeks of eating, as opposed to the meal or two you'll get from the equivalent cut cooked.

If you'd like to learn more about the benefits of premium meat, there is considerable peer-reviewed research confirming the relationship of a pig's diet and breed to the final flavor profile of dry-cured hams.

Acorn-fed pigs are the classic food for the best dry-cured hams, but almost impossible to find.

If you're unsure of where to source good pork, start talking to butchers, farmers, and other pork enthusiasts; in time, you'll find what you're looking for. When I started dry-curing, I was happy to be using pork from a premium national distributor, but I started looking for interesting local meat—local being more important to me than organic. After a few years, I've dry-cured Berkshire-Tamworth pigs raised by my dad; beautiful whey-fed animals raised by the cheesemakers at Jasper Hill Farm; and the legendary woolly Mangalitsa pigs raised by friends at Eastman Farm down the road. It's a bounty of good, local pork, rich with local flavors, and all capable of producing a world-class dry-cured product, but it took time to find. Be patient and you'll eventually come across the quality of pork you're looking for.

As you are searching your region for pork, you may find small farmers who are raising hogs with local food sources—a development I'm very excited about. Near our Oregon home, hazelnut-fed pigs were beginning to appear, and in Vermont whey-fed pigs are becoming common, raised on by-products of the cheese industry and closing an entirely local agricultural loop. With an understanding that the Italian traditions of dry-curing are a critical foundation to build upon, and an awareness that the extensive variety of Mediterranean products is based on locally available resources and environmental conditions, I believe that true authenticity comes not from imitation, but from embracing your local flavors, and creating a product that brings together the complexities and nuances of your home.

Finally, don't be held back by only using pork. Beef, goat, duck, horse, and lamb are all regularly dry-cured, and the basic instructions of this book apply to all. Salami is more difficult to substitute meat other than pork or beef, but for whole-muscle curing, simply find a recipe that looks appealing, and substitute your preferred meat for the pork.

TYPE OF DRY-CURING	MEAT	SALT	TIME	MICROORGANISMS
Whole muscle	Any solid piece of meat	NaCl: 2.5–3.5% Cure #2: 0.25%	2 weeks up to a year	• Mold and yeast on the outside • Staphylococcus bacteria naturally occurring throughout the meat (required for nitrate reduction)
Dry-cured hams (technically a type of whole-muscle dry-curing)	Back leg	NaCl: 3.0–5.0% Cure #2: 0.25%	Year-plus	Same as above
Uncooked, fermented and dried sausage (salami)	Upper shoulder (Boston butt), ham, fatback	NaCl: 2.5–3.5% Cure #2: 0.25%	1–3 days of fermenting; 2 weeks to several months for drying	• Molds and yeasts on the outside • Starter culture of bacteria and yeasts mixed in with the meat and fat

LEARNING HOW TO BUTCHER A PIG

Cutting up a whole pig is the best way to procure ideal cuts and interesting meat for dry-curing. Butchering a pig and trimming meat for dry-curing can be intimidating. Having a good teacher will take the mystery out of the process. Butchering is beyond the scope of this book, but there are many resources available for your education. Begin by looking for classes in your area, as butchering instruction is becoming more common. I learned from Camas Davis at the Portland Meat Collective, and I can't recommend her classes enough. Talk to your butcher, spend some time online looking for videos, and you'll eventually find someone to teach you the process of cutting up a pig, or tricks for trimming meat for dry-curing.

In the meantime, don't let a lack of instruction stop you from cutting up pork. Make sure you have plenty of fridge and freezer space available so you aren't rushed, and start practicing. Experience is as important as instruction, and you might as well start getting your experience right now.

The Salt

The application of salt to meat is the first critical component of dry-cured meats. Salting also includes the addition of nitrates and nitrites, if used.

When people ask what dry-cured pork is, I describe it as "salty, old meat"—a description that not everyone sees as favorable, but I find efficient and accurate, as you can't have dry-cured meat without salt and age. Salt both prevents the growth of unwanted bacteria, and aids in the drying of the meat.

Embrace the saltiness of dry-cured meats, and if you're trying to limit salt in your diet, slice the meat thinly, and consume in moderation. There is a small range of adjustment to salt concentration you can make in the recipes, but as with all preserved foods, important and inflexible guidelines dictate the amount of salt. The recommended guideline is more than 2.6 percent salt in all dry-curing, and 0.25 percent curing salt.

Salt is a primary ingredient and flavor, and using an interesting sea salt will add complexity to your finished product. The different mineral profiles found in sea salts will influence flavor in different ways, so as you refine your recipes, I encourage experimentation with different types of salt. Be aware that some salts contain many impurities, which may remain on the outside of the meat after the salt has been absorbed; just rinse them off, and they shouldn't be a concern.

An alternative to sea salt is Diamond kosher salt, which has a relatively neutral flavor and is inexpensive, easily available, and recommended by many professionals. I often use the brand and I've always been pleased with the results. Unlike Morton kosher salt (which will also work well), Diamond kosher doesn't contain any anti-caking agents. If it isn't available, canning salt is also a pure salt option. Do not use iodized table salt.

CURING SALT

Few ingredients in our food are so ubiquitous yet so maligned as nitrates and nitrites. Commonly referred to as curing salt, and naturally occurring throughout the biological world, including in the human body, nitrates, nitrites, and their related nitrogen-based compounds are among the basic components of the world's nutrient cycles (remember the nitrogen cycle from middle school?). They are critical for our world's functioning ecosystem, and are essential for the safety of many dry-cured meats.

In dry-cured meats, nitrates, nitrites, and their intermediate compounds are responsible for the flavor, color, and, most important, safety of the meat, from the finest Spanish jamon to the lowly gas station meat stick. Regardless of all the other benefits, the fact that curing salt is 100 percent effective in preventing botulism is enough of a reason to include it in all of these recipes.

SALTING AND PRESERVATION

To explain why salt is important for the preservation of meat, first understand that bacteria require water to survive and reproduce; stopping bacteria by removing their access to water is the primary preservation technique of dry-curing. Along with a series of other effects, salting meat will reduce the water available to bacteria, but salt does not actually dry the meat.

To clarify, as the salt dissolves and diffuses through the meat, the salt molecules bind with the water molecules, which makes the water unavailable to bacteria, but without actually removing the water from the meat. A raw, unsalted piece of meat is a damp and ideal environment for bacteria, while a raw, salty piece of meat is still a damp place, but has significantly less water available for bacteria, allowing for short-term preservation as the meat is then dried.

The amount of available water in a piece of meat is more accurately described as "water activity," abbreviated as Aw. Commercial producers closely monitor Aw using digital water activity meters, but observing the weight loss of a drying piece of meat is adequate for the home producer.

It's important to note that the amount of salt

used in dry-curing lowers the water activity enough to provide short-term preservation of the meat, and provides a window of time to dry the meat, but it is not enough salt for long-term preservation. In order to lower Aw enough for long-term preservation, you need to either remove water by drying the meat, or reduce the water activity by heavily salting the meat, like a piece of salt cod or salt-packed anchovies. By employing the drying process in conjunction with salt, you can achieve the long-term preservation of meat without salting beyond palatability.

Curing salt is purchased in a form that resembles standard table salt; it always contains nitrites, and sometimes nitrates. Curing salt is toxic in large quantities, so it is critical to keep it well labeled and out of reach of children. The quantity of curing salt used in all this book's recipes is based on the recommended quantities from the USDA. The USDA's guidelines on curing salt usage are easily found online.

Curing salt is found in two standardized forms in North America, and it's important to understand the difference. Throughout this book I'll refer to two types as either Cure #1 (commonly known as pink salt—it's usually died pink to prevent accidental ingestion), or Cure #2 (which looks like normal salt, so keep it well labeled). Both types are sold under a variety of different names, usually containing a *#1* or *#2*—such as Insta Cure #1, Insta Cure #2, DQ Curing Salt #1 or #2, and Prague Powder #1 or #2. Although rare, you'll occasionally see saltpeter in a recipe for cured meat, and while it has a different chemical composition, it still contains nitrates, so you can substitute Cure #2 for saltpeter.

The difference between Cure #1 and Cure #2 is important. Use Cure #1 for any items that will just be cured and not dried, or for items that will dry rapidly (less than 2 weeks). Only use Cure #2 for items that will be dried for longer than 2 weeks.

To understand the effect nitrates and nitrites have on meat, it's important to first distinguish between them, which may seem obvious, but most people mistakenly treat nitrates and nitrites as interchangeable.

> **NOTE**
>
> Cure #1 contains standard table salt (NaCl) and sodium nitrite ($NaNO_2$), while Cure #2 is salt (NaCl), sodium nitrite ($NaNO_2$), and sodium nitrate ($NaNO_3$).

When added to meat, nitrites (NO_2) immediately undergo a wide range of complex chemical reactions, which eventually convert the nitrite to nitric oxide (NO), leaving very little nitrite remaining in the meat. Nitrites influence color formation (giving cured meats their pink color), flavor formation (a ham doesn't taste like roast pork), they reduce the risk of fat rancidity (which is just the oxidation of lipids over time, but is one of the reasons nitrites are so common in industrially produced foods), and, perhaps most important, they inhibit the bacterium that causes botulism, *Clostridium botulinum*.

In contrast with nitrite, when nitrate (NO_3) is added to meat, it doesn't immediately undergo any relevant chemical reactions; it is important in dry-curing for one key reason: Over time, *Staphylococcus* bacteria—which will naturally populate whole-muscle dry-curing, or are added through the starter culture in a salami—will populate your drying meat and produce the enzyme nitrate reductase, which slowly reduces nitrate into nitrite. This means nitrate is a reservoir of nitrite—providing a long-term supply of it for items that will be dried and aged for long periods of time, including most of the recipes in this book. The rate of conversion from nitrate to nitrite is variable, and giving an exact time for this conversion is impossible. Nitrate is never used on its own, only in conjunction with nitrite (Cure #2 has both types).

Cure #1 and Cure #2 are not interchangeable, and products like Morton's Sugar Cure are not a replacement or adequate substitute for either.

THE SCIENCE OF SALTING

In salami, salt absorption simply happens when you mix all the salt and seasonings into the ground meat and fat. The surface area of the ground meat is high enough that the salt will quickly and easily be absorbed. No special conditions or even further mentions are needed for successfully salting salami.

In whole muscles, salt absorption and distribution may require several weeks, but the process is simple, reliable, and hands-off. Salt absorption and dispersal will take a couple of days for a thin slice of loin, a couple of weeks for a coppa, but might take 2 months for a large bone-in ham.

The key to salting meat is the process of diffusion. If you remember your high school biology, the concept behind diffusion is the tendency for substances to disperse through a substance until an even concentration, or equilibrium, is reached. For example, if you dissolve salt into a glass of water, you won't find pockets of saltier water in the glass—the concentration of salt is equal throughout. The same concept can be applied to meat—given enough moisture in the meat for the salt to dissolve, the salt will disperse

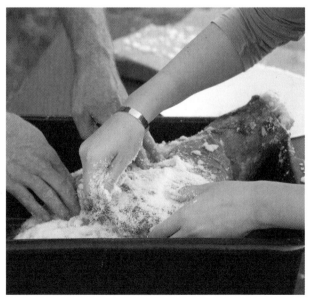

to create an even concentration throughout the meat. (As a side note to those who remember diffusion and osmosis always being taught together, osmosis is also involved in this process, but osmosis is a type of diffusion, and specifically involves movement across a semi-permeable membrane.)

The process looks like this:

First, salt is applied to the outside of the meat and begins dissolving into the layer of moisture coating the meat. The dissolved salt starts to migrate from the area of high concentration (the salty outside of the meat) to the area of low concentration (the interior).

At the same time, the water inside the meat (a high concentration of water) starts migrating to the salty layer on the outside (a low concentration of water). This results in moisture leaving the meat. Not enough moisture is lost for any significant drying of the meat.

What then follows is a back-and-forth of salt and water. Salt goes in, water goes out, but as the salt concentration increases inside the meat, the water "follows" the salt back in, and everything keeps moving around, slowly reaching equilibrium.

If you're salting a piece of meat in a plastic bag, and one day you notice lots of liquid in the bag, then return a few days later to find it relatively dry, it's because the water was reabsorbed by the meat as the interior became more salty.

If you're salting the meat on a rack, as opposed to in a bag, the exuded liquid cannot be reabsorbed, so you have less moisture remaining in the meat at the end of the process, and the drying process may be a little quicker. You'll see this in the recipe for dry-cured hams.

As the salt is being absorbed, it's important to keep the meat cold to limit bacterial growth. Keep the salted meat under 40°F, and if it's in a sealed bag, you don't need to worry about humidity, but if it's open in the low-humidity environment of your fridge, it may start to dry out, which will limit the ability for the salt to move freely—I suggest covering the container that holds the meat with plastic wrap.

It's impossible for me to tell you exactly how long this process will take, but if you use a precise weight of salt, there is no threat of oversalting, so I'll usually leave meat for 3 weeks (ham is the exception, and it's detailed in its own section).

THE FACTS ABOUT NITRATES

To address the health concerns around nitrites and nitrates directly, there are several important facts. First, both will break down to their harmless components if aged properly. For recipes using only nitrites, this may take just a couple of days of curing and resting; for recipes using nitrites and nitrates, the timing is more variable, but occurs as the meat hangs and dries. To speed this process, commercial bacon producers use a curing accelerator, usually ascorbic acid, or sodium erythorbate, which increases the speed of the various curing reactions and the breakdown of nitrite. The use of a curing accelerator assures that very few residual nitrites are left in the meat; if you are concerned about nitrites remaining in your bacon, pancetta, or guanciale (all products that are usually cooked), use a curing accelerator to speed their breakdown. Nitrates are only a concern as they will eventually break down into nitrites.

With this background knowledge, the specific health concern surrounding nitrites is that potentially carcinogenic compounds are created when cured meat, containing residual nitrites, is burned. These compounds, called nitrosamines, are only a concern for those people who like their bacon burnt. If there are no remaining nitrites, and you do not burn your bacon, these compounds will not form.

Finally, if your concern is that nitrites and nitrates are unnatural preservatives, be aware that they are found in high levels in most leafy green vegetables (spinach contains large quantities) throughout the natural world, as well as in heart medications, desensitizing toothpaste, and—most important for our world's population—fertilizer. The nitrites and nitrates found in curing salts are created through an industrial process (the same process as fixing nitrogen for fertilizer). If you prefer to use a natural source of nitrites and nitrates, vegetable powder substitutes are available from most sausage supply companies (be aware that the nitrites and nitrates in these powders most likely originated from a industrially made fertilizer—they've simply been passed through a plant before arriving in your kitchen).

If you choose to avoid nitrites, please take the time to research their importance in more detail before removing them from any recipe. Under no circumstances can salami be safely made without nitrites. Any labeling of commercial salamis that says "uncured" or "made without additional nitrites or nitrates" is misleading. Those salamis do contain nitrites; they're just added through vegetable powder, instead of in a pure form (this goes for "uncured" hot dogs and bacon as well). The misleading packaging is a result of a flaw in the USDA's extensive regulation of cured meats. Some producers use "uncured" as a marketing tool, but others would prefer not to mislead consumers—yet their hands are tied by labeling restrictions.

COLD-SMOKING

Whenever cold-smoking dry-cured meats, you must use curing salt. Without nitrite, botulism is a concern due to the mild temperatures and oxygen-free environment created by the smoke.

The majority of smoked meat most of us are familiar with is hot-smoked. The hot smoke slowly cooks and tenderizes the meat, and the result is items such as beef brisket, pulled pork, bacon, ribs, and so on.

In cold-smoking, though, the temperature of the smoke stays below 90°F. Cold-smoking is the only appropriate method for smoking dry-cured meats, and is also used when smoking cheese and some fish. In the past, cold-smoking required contraptions that cooled the smoke before it reached the food, which kept all but the most dedicated from cold-smoking.

You can now buy a simple cold-smoke generator for about $40. These make the process foolproof, and are used by both serious hobbyists and professionals. The A-Maze-N Smoker and the ProQ Cold Smoke Generator are available.

There's nothing complicated about the way cold-smoke generators work—and the result is a real hardwood smoke. The smoke is produced by slowly smoldering a maze of sawdust, and they release so little heat that you can easily smoke your meat in a cardboard box. Bags of sawdust are cheap and avail-able in many types of wood. One bag will provide enough sawdust for many sessions of smoking.

Experiment with the length of cold-smoking, and find a level that suits you. I usually smoke items for 2 or 3 days, but some people go for a week. You can always apply a second round for a stronger flavor.

Take into consideration when in the process you'll be smoking the meat. I smoke salami right after fermentation is over (but I let the casing dry a little to better absorb the smoke), and I smoke whole muscles after I've removed them from the salt, and cased and trussed the meat. In both these scenarios I risk drying the outside layer of the meat too much; my assumption is that the meat is so moist at this point, a little extra drying won't hurt. You can also rig a system to smoke while you ferment salami, but I haven't bothered.

A few final thoughts: You can smoke any dry-cured product, so don't be held back by recipes. Smoking will stop most mold from growing, so don't bother inoculating your meat. Finally, keep in mind the outside temperature as you cold-smoke. You're at the mercy of the weather: If the temperature drops below freezing, or it gets hot, you're going to have some problems (your meat might freeze or spoil). This rules out smoking in midsummer or midwinter for me, so I usually cold-smoke in the fall, when the temperature is reliably cool.

Time

Dry-cured meats take time, and temperature and humidity can be critical during this time, although not all dry-curing requires precision.

Drying is the longest, and sometimes most difficult, part of the process. Drying is needed to preserve the meat, as unwanted bacteria can't tolerate a dry environment, but it's also where the flavors are created and concentrated. Drying is when the textures develop, and it's when you either create a showcase of the meat, worthy of the weeks or months of waiting, or are left with a hard salty block—or worse, a rotten, raw piece of meat that you've waited months for, just to throw away.

The standard amount of drying time is until 30 percent of the original weight has been lost, but dry to your personal preferences. Drier is not necessarily better—your products will have better flavor, seem less salty, have a better texture, and slice more easily if they still have some moisture remaining.

As you get started, learn the temperature and humidity around your house, and choose your recipes based on those conditions. The farther you are from ideal temperature and humidity (55°F, 75 percent relative humidity), the thinner the meat you should dry-cure—and if it's really hot, you can dry thin slices in your fridge. Start small, and with each success, consider drying something larger. Keep in mind that one of the reasons people around the world preserved their meat in different ways is because they had to adapt to the drying conditions of their local environment. The Mediterranean region is renowned for its products because it has ideal drying conditions.

The goal for any piece of meat is a slow and steady rate of drying, as this gives time for the enzymes to break down the nitrates, proteins, and amino acids, creating new flavors and increasing complexity. The amount of time varies; a big coppa may take a few months, while a small coppa might only take 6 weeks. The longer an item dries (without overdrying), the more complex a flavor profile it will have, but you don't want to dry the meat so slowly that it rots. One reason prosciutto is so flavorful is that after the ham has dried properly, lard is smeared all over the exposed flesh, preventing any more moisture loss. It's then aged for many more months, allowing for a great variety of flavors to develop.

> ## NOTE
>
> To calculate the amount of weight lost, divide the final weight by the starting weight, and multiply by 100. This will tell you the percentage of weight remaining—70 percent remaining weight equals a 30 percent weight loss.

THE SCIENCE OF DRYING AND AGING

Drying occurs because water evaporates from the outer surface of the hanging meat. The goal is to balance the rate of evaporation from the outer layer with the rate of the moisture migrating from the inner layer to the outer. If the moisture in the outer layer evaporates too quickly, the moisture deep inside won't move to the outside quickly enough, and you'll get a hard crust around the outside of the meat. This can lock in the remaining interior moisture, and spoilage bacteria may have enough time to take hold, causing rot. Consider all the following variables in your drying, but perfect control of each is not necessary.

- **Surface area** The greater the surface area of meat, the faster it will dry. A deboned ham (speck) will dry much faster than a bone-in ham (prosciutto) because of its exposed flesh. Thin, wide, and flat cuts dry the fastest—focus on these if you have less-than-ideal drying conditions.

- **Casing** Putting whole muscles in large sausage casings will regulate their drying, keep their outside layer from getting too hard, and generally improve the product.

- **Airspeed** You want air movement in your drying space, but it's easy to overdo it. Too much air movement and you'll quickly harden the outside layer of the drying meat. I use a very small, weak computer fan, and point it away from the meat. Ideally I just want a slow recirculation of air every few hours, but I've underestimated the effect of a fan before, and accidentally dried some things too quickly resulting in a hard crust.

- **Humidity** Humidity is probably the hardest variable for people to control, but with available humidity controllers, it shouldn't be any more difficult than temperature. Be aware that relative humidity is difficult to measure accurately. After some testing, I found that it's not uncommon for cheap humidity meters to be 5 to 10 percent off. You can purchase humidity calibration bags online inexpensively.

- **Temperature** Temperature is more important for enzyme activity than drying, but enzyme activity is important. Enzymes break down amino acids to create more flavor, and they break down nitrates to nitrites. Low temperatures inhibit enzymes. A good average temperature for drying meat is 55°F—but a little higher or lower is absolutely fine. My drying space cools to 48°F in the winter, and I've never noticed any negative effect.

Controlling Your Environmental Conditions

The optimum environment for drying meat is a dark place with sustained temperatures between 50 and 55°F, and a relative humidity of 65 to 75 percent. I dry at 55°F and 75 percent relative humidity.

While unnecessary for drying thin and flat items, having control over your environmental conditions is critical for fridge drying large items, and will dramatically improve the quality and chances of success with all your dry-curing. It also gives you control of a key variable and allows for repeatability and fine-tuning of your recipes.

Anywhere you dry, even a temperature- and humidity-controlled space, will have its own cycles and fluctuations, which is fine, and unavoidable. In any drying space, fresh air should be introduced regularly, and if space allows it, a slow movement of air around the chamber is ideal (if you can feel a breeze, it's too much—it's very easy for a fan to overdry the outside of your meat).

There are three approaches for managing your drying environment.

1. A PASSIVE APPROACH

Get to know the temperature and humidity in different dark places around your home, and choose projects based on your conditions, moving the meat as needed. Think ahead and keep in mind how the conditions will change over the weeks/months of drying time. For example, 2 weeks ago my basement was 50°F and 50 percent relative humidity—today it's 10 degrees warmer and there's a river running through it.

2. ACTIVE TEMPERATURE CONTROL, PASSIVE HUMIDITY CONTROL

This is probably the most common technique for controlling your environment, and uses a fridge for maintaining the desired temperature, and a pan of salt-saturated water for humidity control. With a purchased temperature controller, any fridge can be adjusted to any temperature, without modification to the fridge.

An under-counter fridge works well for this, as it's a small space to humidify, and unlike a normal fridge it doesn't have an unnecessary freezer. A dorm-style fridge can work, but will be too short for most items. Wine fridges may have the advantage of precise temperature control built in.

Begin by learning how warm your fridge will run—turn the cold adjuster as warm as it gets, put a thermometer inside, and let it go. Check the temperature regularly over a couple of days; if you're lucky, it'll be up near 50 to 55°F. If not, purchase a temperature controller (simply a plug-in thermostat), available from any homebrewing store.

Maintaining a 75 percent relative humidity in a small space is simple. When water is saturated with salt, it will naturally create an environment of 75 percent humidity. The mixture won't influence the flavors of the meat, and the high salt concentration will prevent weird molds and bacteria from growing in the water.

To create the humidity, use the widest container that will fit in the fridge, and dissolve salt into warm water until it is saturated. Put the salt/water mixture in the fridge, and monitor both temperature and humidity for a few days before you put any meat in the space.

One of the potential problems with this technique is the dehydrating nature of a fridge. If the outside temperature is warm, and the fridge is running its compressor frequently, the salt/water mixture may not be able to keep up with the dehydration of the fridge, and the humidity will drop. Most fridges are efficient enough that this shouldn't be a problem anywhere but the hottest climates.

3. ACTIVE TEMPERATURE CONTROL, ACTIVE HUMIDITY CONTROL

In the long run, you're going to want a space where you can control both temperature and humidity. It's simple, and it gives you complete control and repeatability in your process. There are countless ways of creating a temperature- and humidity-controlled space; what I'm presenting is just one option.

The required equipment is: a fridge or other cooling space (I have a room with an AC unit built in—detailed below), a temperature controller (I use Ranco brand), a humidity controller, a thermometer, and an analog humidifier.

As mentioned above, you might be able to buy a wine fridge with temperature control, but the cheaper option is buying an old fridge and a temperature controller. Homebrewers use these to control the temperature of fermenting beer; they're easy to use and allow for both heating and cooling settings.

The way temperature controllers work is by turning on or off the power to the fridge, based on your programmed temperature and the temperature of a sensor you place inside. You plug the fridge into the controller, then plug the controller into a normal power outlet and run a wire with a temperature sensor on the end through the door of the fridge. If this isn't clear, it will be when it's in your hands—it's really simple.

Humidity is controlled in the same manner, with a humidity controller (humidistat) placed inside the fridge, and an analog humidifier plugged into it. The most difficult aspect of humidity control is running electricity into your fridge for power. The skin of a fridge is filled with coils; if you drill a hole in the side, you risk puncturing a coil, which will ruin the fridge. The easiest method is to just run power through a crack in the door.

An alternative option is a humidifier with built in humidistat. This is an all-in-one unit that lets you set a specific desired humidity level. Not all adjustable humidifiers will let you set a humidity level as high

as 65 to 75 percent, so confirm this before purchasing. You'll still need to run power into the fridge.

Once you have power inside, plug the humidity controller in, and plug the humidifier into the controller. Be aware that humidity meters and humidity controllers have a tendency to be inaccurate. You can buy cheap little humidity meters, used by cigar aficionados, that you can calibrate, and will provide you with an accurate reference point.

The use of an analog, not a digital, humidifier is important, as the humidity controller works by turning on and off power. Many digital humidifiers need you to manually press an "on" button after power has been turned off—as opposed to an analog humidifier, which has a physical "on" switch, and will remain on regardless of power being turned on and off.

AND SO ON . . .

After going through a series of curing/drying chambers, most recently we've built a small, climate-controlled room in the basement. Our old fridge has turned into a dedicated salami and beer fermenting space, and the room in the basement has become a community drying room. If you've got a group of interested people, or are just dry-curing a whole pig each fall, I recommend building a dedicated space. It was easy to build, uses an old AC unit to maintain very steady temperature, along with a basic humidifier. It's well insulated so that the room can be turned down cold enough to serve as a walk-in fridge if we need it (we keep uncut primals cold in it as we work our way through butchering the pigs in the fall).

If building a structure like this is interesting

lets, there is a source of dedicated power to run the humidity controller and a small computer fan (which caused too-fast drying problems at first). For fresh-air intake, there is a bathroom fan in the ceiling, controlled by a 24-hour timer. The air intake has a filter on it, in the hope of reducing the quantity of molds being pulled into the chamber—but I don't know if that's possible in a Vermont basement in the middle of summer. For temperature control I use a digital dual-stage Ranco controller; I purchased the humidity controller from a greenhouse supply store.

LEARN YOUR CHAMBER

Every chamber has its own personality. Get a wireless thermometer/humidity meter, and watch how the temperature and humidity fluctuate over time. I used to worry about keeping everything ultra-precise, but have since realized that perfect precision is not necessary, or even possible; as long as I'm staying within the ideal range, the results will be good.

Preparing Your Meat For Drying

While casing is obviously required when making salami, the use of large sausage casings when drying whole muscles will improve your final quality: It regulates drying, prevents the formation of a crust around the outside layer, and allows for easy removal of mold. That being said, casing whole muscles is not required; it's also not possible with flat cuts of meat. Any meat that is dried uncased can still be excellent. Remember to always remove the casing before eating any dry-cured meats—salami included.

to you, consult the many DIY walk-in cooler builds available online. Homebrewing sites are a good place to start; you'll simply need to add humidity into the equation. You may need to override the AC unit's thermostat to get a cool temperature, but if you're willing to build a whole room for aging meat, I'm guessing you can figure that out.

It probably cost us $600 total to build our room, and this includes paying a friend to do the initial framing. With the framing in place, we installed rigid foam insulation, keeping in mind the potential for condensation where the insulation joined, and resulting mold problems in the summer. Cooling is done through an old AC unit, which is plugged into one of two pairs of temperature-controlled outlets, one for cooling and one for heating (which we've never used). In addition to the temperature-controlled out-

NATURAL VERSUS SYNTHETIC

Casings come in natural and synthetic versions, and within each of these categories there is extensive variation. Synthetic casings have the advantage of being uniform and odor-free, with an indefinite shelf life. Natural casings will last for over a year in salt (or longer); they give a natural and traditional look to your product and adhere well to the meat. Natural casings can be variable in their size and shape. Some people are put off by the smell of natural casings, but this quickly goes away with adequate rinsing in fresh water. We exclusively use natural casings, for all of the above reasons. In addition, I find that they stretch well; and for large or abnormally shaped items, natural casings are easy to close by sewing with a needle and thread.

Certain types of dry-curing are traditionally tied to specific casings. For example, culatello is cased in a beef bladder (there is no synthetic casing that will hold a culatello), and 'nduja and sopressata are traditionally cased in hog middles. While a different casing might not change the flavor, if you're trying to emulate a specific region's traditions, you'll need to consider the type of casing.

CASING PREPARATION

Follow the manufacturer's or retailer's recommendations for both synthetic and natural casings. Generally, natural casings need to be rinsed of salt, and the inside and outside washed and soaked in cold water. Begin by unraveling the desired amount (always prepare more than you think you will need—running out of casing is anger inducing), and then run cold water through the inside of the casings. Do this in a large container, as the casings have a tendency to flop out into your bacteria-covered sink. After a thorough rinse of the interior, soak the entire casing in cold water for a few hours, or overnight (change the water several times). You'll notice that any smell associated with the casing dissipates with rinsing. Before using, a quick rinse in warm water will make the casings more pliable.

I've often forgotten to prep my casings ahead of time, and just rinsed them in cold water for a few min-

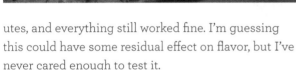

utes, and everything still worked fine. I'm guessing this could have some residual effect on flavor, but I've never cared enough to test it.

TYPES OF NATURAL CASINGS

The following are the most commonly used casings.

Salami

- Beef middles: The standard salami casing. Beef middles will have a straight shape and are about 2½ inches in diameter.

- Hog casings: The standard casing used for fresh sausage, hog casings will quickly dry into a thin salami. They are a good size if your drying conditions are not optimal. Hog casings are curved.

- Genoa sack: A specialty casing sold by Butcher & Packer Supply Company, and used to make Genoa salami.

- Hog middles: A large hog casing traditionally used to make 'nduja and sopressata.

Whole Muscles

- Beef bung cap: My most-used casing, beef bungs are large and thus ideal for casing coppa, loin, fiocca, or any other chunks of whole muscle. Beef bungs are closed on one end, and have a small hole a few inches from the opening. You can dry salami in a beef bung, but it will be a large salami, and you need careful humidity control. Beef bungs come in a variety of sizes, and I always keep several in the fridge. They adhere well to the meat, so if you use one that's too big, just truss well, and it'll work fine.

- Beef bladder: Traditional for culatello, a beef bladder can be difficult to source. When used with culatello they are cut lengthwise and then sewed around the meat, using a trussing needle and twine. Butcher & Packer sells an air-dried bladder that will work as a substitute.

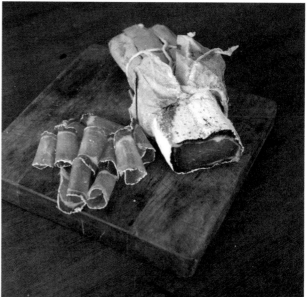

THE BROWN BAG OPTION

I've seen people case whole muscles in brown paper bags trussed tightly around the meat. I tested this method on a few different items, and while it worked, there was quite a bit of mold growth under the bag. Fortunately the mold wasn't anything I was worried about, as our drying chamber has a healthy population of desireable mold, and the meat tasted great, but I don't know if the bag actually accomplished anything. One benefit was being able to roll the meat in cracked pepper before wrapping in the brown paper (the pepper would have scraped off when I shoved it in a standard casing).

Tying and Trussing

The tying and trussing of your cured meats is important for functional and aesthetic reasons. The meat needs to be hanging to dry, and trussing it into a uniform shape will aid in even drying. There are many approaches to tying and trussing a piece of meat. Expect a messy and inefficient process at first, which will become routine with some practice.

As an alternative to trussing your meat, elastic tubular netting is a tool allowing you to create a uniform and professional-looking final product easily. To use, slip the netting over the cased meat, tie the ends, and hang as usual.

Before proceeding, spend time watching online instructional videos of tying and trussing roasts, sausages, and salami, as a video will be more useful than a written description.

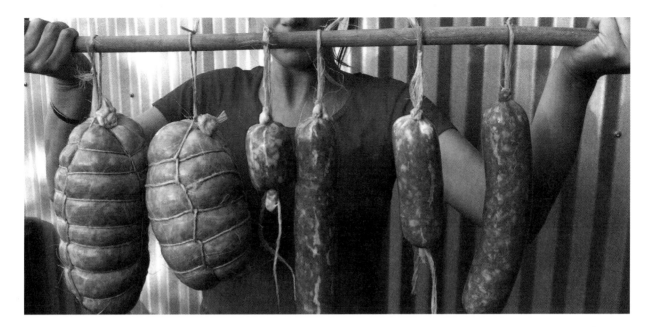

One difficult aspect of tying meat to hang is tying a knot that will not drop the heavy meat and slimy casing. On a couple of occasions I've checked on my drying meat the day after hanging, only to find the salami or coppa lying on the floor of the chamber. There are many different methods for tying a secure knot; I use a technique that Ruhlman and Polcyn call a "bubble knot."

To tie this knot, first find a partner who will hold the casing tight to the meat, or—as Paul Bertolli recommends—use locking forceps to clamp the end of the casing tightly. Once the casing is closed tightly against the meat, use your butcher's twine to tie the first half of a surgeon's knot as close to the meat as possible. When that knot is tight, tie a half hitch around the casing, about ½ inch away from the initial knot. There will be a "bubble" between the two knots,

which should be a good start to preventing the meat from dropping. There are many good online tutorials for tying a surgeon's knot and half hitch.

If you're trussing the meat, leave a long tail of butcher's twine, or tie a new length of string to the casing and tie a series of half-hitches down and around the length of the meat. The trussing is critical to preventing the meat from falling, but it doesn't need to be pretty. Make sure you have a loop of twine running under the hanging end of the meat to hold the weight; otherwise trust that you'll develop your own efficient and attractive process with practice.

Like I said, a video makes it easier, so start looking online. Everybody has their own style of tying and trussing; don't worry about learning the one authentic or correct method. Practice, and expect this to take longer than you expect.

WHY AGING MAKES SOME FOODS TASTE BETTER
(THE ANSWER IS ALWAYS ENZYMES)

According to Fidel Toldra's 2002 book *Dry-Cured Meat Products*, over 200 different volatile compounds have been identified as contributing to the flavor and aroma of aged Spanish, Italian, and French dry-cured hams, and more than 150 to a dry-cured salami. Ham aromas and flavors have been likened to mushrooms, pineapple, crackers, caramel, nuts, sweat, sulfur, cocoa, cheese, grass, lilies, wine, toasted onion, and even dirty socks. The complexity of properly aged dry-cured meat is unparalleled in any fresh pork. A young dry-cured ham will show significantly less flavor complexity than one aged for a year or more. The primary source of this complexity of flavor is the slow degrading of proteins, amino acids, lipids, and other components of the muscle by a variety of enzymes.

If you're unfamiliar with enzymes and what they do, enzymes are specialized protein molecules that help build up or break down molecules. Without enzymes, life couldn't exist. Enzymes are the catalyst for so many biological processes that I used to tell my biology students to just write "enzyme" whenever they couldn't remember an answer on a test. That was actually terrible advice, but you get the idea.

Enzymes are interesting molecules, as they require no energy to do their job, they are produced in the cells of all living organisms, they are not alive, and while some will degrade very quickly, others can continue to function for years after the organism that produced them has died.

Several groups of enzymes are of importance to dry-curing—including nitrate reductase, responsible for converting nitrate to nitrite, and supplied by Staphylococcus bacteria (which will naturally populate all dry-cured meats but is found in the starter culture used to make salami)—but it's the endogenous enzymes, produced within the muscle while the pig was still alive, that are responsible for the development of flavor compounds as meat ages. (Salami is an exception, as there are many different things happening as a result of the added starter culture.)

Meat is full of protein, protein is made of peptides, peptides are made of amino acids, and so on. Protein is not a complex flavor on its own—think of a pork chop—but when broken apart, the components of a protein are flavorful and aromatic. As meat ages, the long-lasting, very slow-acting enzymes present in it will slowly start breaking apart the proteins into these smaller pieces.

Amino acids and peptides are found in increasing number as a dry-cured hams age. Certain specific amino acids and peptides give long-aged hams their traditional flavors, and from this it's easy to see how longer aging results in a more complex product. Peptides, amino acids, and their components are a primary source of flavor and aroma, but numerous other important reactions influence flavor, especially involving the breakdown of lipids. The countless number of variations is overwhelming, and while it's beyond our means to control all the variables, feeding a pig a balanced and healthy diet is a good place to start.

Finally, understand that a discussion of flavor development can quickly enter the realm of meat-science dissertations. What I'm presenting is only a fraction of what is going on as meat ages.

Microorganisms (Mold)

All dry-cured meats are populated with an ecosystem of microorganisms, which are responsible for many of the characteristics of dry-cured meats. You may feel nervous about encouraging mold on a food that you're ultimately going to eat, but if you want delicious dry-cured meats, you'll need to embrace microorganisms as an important part of the process.

Without the use of chemicals to inhibit their growth, an ecosystem of mold, yeast, and bacteria will populate the outside of all drying meat. While yeast and bacteria are always present, and a salami relies on an entire ecosystem of microorganisms, mold is what you will spend most of your time managing on any piece of drying meat. As undesirable mold can be very toxic, mold management is an unavoidable part of the dry-curing process. Unwanted mold can be controlled through vigilant removal from the meat with a vinegar-soaked towel.

While you'll usually find only a handful of different species of mold populating any piece of meat, the range of possible species is significant. *Penicillium nalgiovense* is the standard salami mold, with its growth easily promoted with a purchased starter culture, but it's just one of 300 diverse molds found in the *Penicillium* genus. The *Penicillium* molds are a very important group, not just in dry-curing, but also in cheesemaking and

the production of chemicals; perhaps most important, they are the original source of penicillin, the first antibiotic. Fortunately, *Penicillium nalgiovense* produces penicillin in such low quantities that the mold coating a piece of dry-cured meat is not a concern to those with penicillin allergies.

USING A MOLD CULTURE

The easiest, and recommended way of controlling the growth and species of mold on your dry-curing is through the use of a purchased mold culture. The most common mold culture is Bactoferm Mold 600, produced by Chr. Hansen, which contains a

freeze-dried culture of *Penicillium nalgiovense*. This culture will produce a traditional flat, white mold that, when applied correctly, will outcompete most undesirable molds. A healthy layer of desirable mold will also have the advantage of slowing the drying process, allowing for more flavor development. And it will contribute its own flavors, aspects of which you may recognize from other dry-cured meats and many cheeses. In addition to these influences, certain molds will reduce the acidity of the outside layer of salami.

Apply the mold culture to the meat after casing, but before any drying or fermentation has occurred. Follow the instructions of the manufacturer to rehydrate the mold in distilled water, and then apply the mold with a spray bottle or dip the meat into the culture. I recommend filling a wide and shallow baking dish with a thin layer of the rehydrated culture, then rolling the meat in the liquid. In a couple of days, this should produce a healthy population of white mold on the meat without wasting too much of the culture.

If you are cold-smoking your meat, the smoke will inhibit most mold growth, and using a mold culture is unnecessary.

While many commercial producers encourage controlled mold growth during the drying of their salamis, the white coating found on most purchased salami is often not mold but rather rice flour or a similar white flour/powder. In these cases, either the mold coating has been removed—mold growth can be unpredictable over time and doesn't hold up to packaging well—or no mold was ever allowed to

grow. In both cases, the salami is rolled in the rice flour to maintain the traditional white, powdery appearance.

POPULATIONS OF MOLD

If left alone, with no added mold culture, your meat may naturally become coated in a nice white, powdery, flat layer of mold. For those of us who work hard to cultivate our local flavors, this can seem like an ideal development, and something to be encouraged. While many people will tell you this mold is okay, the reality is that any unknown mold, regardless of what

mycotoxins can be slow acting, with no feedback indicating their ability to cause harm—the fact you don't get sick after eating a mold doesn't mean that regular consumption will not have long-term effects.

As a follow-up question, I inquired about the safety of slicing off the outer layer of meat to remove the mold. Mold requires oxygen to grow, and the interior of any drying meat is relatively oxygen-free, so this is a somewhat effective method, but again, without knowledge of specific mold species, it is impossible to say if this is a safe option.

European scientists have studied in detail the mold that populates aging foods, but each region's molds are different, and in the United States the research is not as detailed. Without this specific background knowledge about indigenous mold species, I am unable to recommend the promotion of local mold species on your dry-cured meat.

PREVENTING MOLD GROWTH WITH A MOLD INHIBITOR

As an alternative to using a purchased mold culture, you can prevent mold and yeast growth with the use of potassium sorbate, which is a common mold inhibitor and food preservative. Potassium sorbate can be purchased from sausage supply companies; use it according to the manufacturer's recommendations. It's made using standard industrial manufacturing methods, and is not available in naturally occurring forms. Although potassium sorbate is commonly used in many foods and drinks, there are potentially serious health concerns surrounding its use.

it looks like, carries potential risk.

To learn more about the negative effects of unknown molds, I contacted Benjamin Wolfe, who has made a name for himself through his writing, teaching, and research concerning the ecosystems of microbes inhabiting various foodstuffs.

The concern with unknown molds is that different molds produce a wide range of toxins, specifically called mycotoxins, and mycotoxins can have severe and long-lasting effects, which may or may not be immediately noticeable. Unlike the immediate feedback you get from eating spoiled food, certain

Equipment

WHAT YOU NEED TO GET STARTED

Scale

You may need two scales, a precise scale (0.1g) for weighing curing salt and other ingredients, and a higher-capacity version for large pieces of meat. Small digital scales can be found for less than $20. Hanging scales are convenient for large hams (20 to 30 pounds), but they're not as accurate for smaller items.

Butcher's Twine

To hang, tie, and truss your meat. Hemp or linen is traditional, but I use a standard cotton butcher's twine.

Meat Lugs

Plastic food-service containers used to hold meat. Have a few of these on hand—you will find many ways to use them.

Thermometer and Humidity Meter

These two components can be found combined in digital units for $10 at hardware stores or big-box stores. Buy this soon, and start learning the temperature and relative humidity where you might want to dry your meat. Humidity is difficult to monitor accurately, so don't assume you're getting an exact reading; you will get a general idea, though.

Knives

Some people feel strongly about their knives, but for most meat cutting I use cheap boning knives, usually with a curved, flexible blade, which I buy from restaurant supply stores for less than $20. I also have a nice big scimitar for breaking down carcasses. Keep a sharpening steel by your side at all times and keep your knives sharp.

Casing Pricker

This pokes holes in the casing on a salami or whole muscle. A needle sterilized in a flame works well, but it's slow.

Curved Needle and Thread

A curved needle, or trussing needle, and thread are helpful for sewing up casings that have ripped, or have been cut to accommodate a large piece of meat (like a culatello).

Slicer

Every dry-cured pork enthusiast should own a slicer. You'll get perfect, paper-thin slices every time, making serving easier. Thin slices are also important to fully appreciate the texture and flavor of your final product.

WHAT YOU NEED FOR SALAMI

Meat Grinder
Grinder attachments for food processors will work, but are slow compared with purpose-built meat grinders.

Meat Mixer
For mixing the ingredients in a sausage or salami. You don't need one—we don't use one—but it'll make life easier, especially with large batches of salami.

Sausage Stuffer
The quality of sausage stuffer can make a big difference in how long the process of making sausage and salami takes. Do not use the stuffer attachment for a food processor, as it will overwork the meat.

OTHER HELPFUL TOOLS

Wireless Temperature and Humidity Meter

This will allow you to check on temperature and humidity without opening your curing and drying chamber. Highly recommended, and get one that records minimum and maximum temperature and humidity.

Meat Thermometer

When making salami, you want to keep a close eye on the temperature of meat and fat. The Thermapen is a widely loved digital thermometer, and I can't recommend it enough. It's quick and very accurate, and I'm always finding new uses for it.

Cold-Smoker

See more detail on page 29. The A-Maze-N Smoker or Pro-Q Cold Smoke Generator are both cheap, easy, and effective cold-smokers.

Vacuum Sealer

A vacuum sealer is great for bagging meat during the salting and curing stage, as it removes any risk of liquid leaking all over your fridge, and keeps the salt in contact with the meat. Additionally, once your meat has finished drying, vacuum sealing and then freezing is the best way to keep dry-curing fresh, if you're not eating it right away. I've seen a dramatic improvement by freezing in a vacuum-sealed bag rather than a zip-close version.

Temperature Controller

This is simply a plug-in thermostat, and it's essential to precise temperature control of a refrigerator (it's also helpful for salami fermentation). Digital controllers can be found for not much more than analog versions, and allow for more precision. They're available at most online homebrew supply stores. I use Ranco brand. This is a tool you could use more than one of—I have four.

Humidity Controller (Humidistat)

This device controls humidity by turning on or off power to a humidifier. They can be found at greenhouse supply stores. You don't need one if your humidifier is able to be set to a precise humidity.

Humidifier

Either buy one with built-in humidity control, or buy a humidifier that will stay on regardless of power being cut and then restored—that's how a humidity controller regulates the humidity.

Drying Chamber

Ideally you need a space below 60°F, and close to 70 to 75 percent humidity, with some variation being acceptable. For more details, see page 114.

Fermentation chamber

You can ferment salami in a variety of places, but if you're serious about making it, you'll want a space in which you can control the temperature (and it needs to be humid). See more on page 113.

HOW TO USE THESE RECIPES—
UNITS AND MEASURING

All quantities of ingredients are given as a percentage of weight instead of teaspoons, tablespoons, or cups. Salt, and especially curing salt, is a powerful ingredient, with very small amounts being used; the only way to get accurate quantities is with the use of a precise scale.

The recipes in this book use grams as the unit of weight when measuring. You can use ounces if you prefer, but by using grams you can avoid the messiness that comes with trying to figure out fractions

CURING SALT

Many of these recipes call for salt cure, which is a table salt to which sodium nitrite has been added (called Cure #1) or to which both sodium nitrate and sodium nitrate has been added (called Cure #2). Nitrite blocks the growth of botulism-causing bacteria and prevents spoilage. You don't want to cure meat without it. The percentages of these salts are much lower in the recipes, as you don't need as much. So when you're doing your math, remember that .25% becomes .0025. Be careful and double-check your work.

of ounces. Precise gram scales can be found for relatively low prices (order online, look at your local coffee shop or homebrewing store, or—as one guy said to me—go to the place where you buy your Jimi Hendrix posters).

You might be aging some of these recipes for 6 months or a year, so it's worth taking the time to making sure the amounts are exact. In addition, if you want to perfect a recipe to your individual tastes, you are going to need precise measurements that are easily replicated and modified, even a year or two later. Be warned that many precise gram scales will not be strong enough to weigh large pieces of meat—an accurate kitchen scale is better suited for that task. Best to have both on hand.

In order to use these recipes, you're going to need to use a small amount of math. As a math teacher, I hope I can make this process clear to all. The amounts for each ingredient are given as a percentage of the meat's weight. For example, maybe you want to use an amount of salt equal to 3 percent of the total weight of meat. If the meat weighs 2,500 grams, which is about 5 pounds, that means 75 grams of salt, which is about ¼ cup.

Practice this, and I'm going to give the standard and usually ignored math teacher advice here—show

CALCULATING MEASUREMENTS

Step One: Convert percentage to decimal (move point two places to the left, so 3% would be .03 and .25% becomes .0025.

Step Two: You need to figure out the weight of that percentage of the meat. So you'll need to multiply the weight of the meat by that percentage (now a decimal). So to find out what 3% of a 2,500 gram piece of meat (about five pounds) equals, multiply 2,500 x .03. The answer is 75 grams.

Step Three: Weigh out 75 grams of salt and go from there. If you want to be able to eyeball your ingredients and make sure you're on the right track, look at the chart that shows you about how much salt (or meat, or spices) is in a 75 grams (or whatever amount you're trying to weigh).

your work. By putting the equation down on paper, you will improve your accuracy, be able to review your calculations, and have a record of your recipes. Finally—and this is my second frequently ignored math teacher advice—check your work. It might be months of waiting before you get to taste your dry-curing, and you want to make sure you calculated the salt and curing salt correctly. Careless mistakes are easy to make, and you don't want to accidentally add 30 percent salt instead of 3 percent.

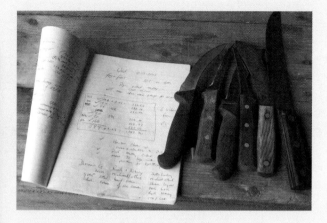

WHAT DOES 2,500 GRAMS LOOK LIKE? OR, THE EQUIVALENT VOLUME MEASUREMENTS

If you don't have a scale, it is possible to make some of these recipes using volume measurements, but only when the recipe calls for table salt. We do not recommend this method when using curing salt because those salts are too concentrated to measure accurately without a scale.

Conversions that will help you to picture the amounts of each ingredient.

Meat
1 pound meat = 454 grams

Spices/herbs
1 teaspoon = 2 grams

Salt
For the recipes in which I give volume measurements, I used Morton's Kosher.

When you measure by volume, each type of salt has a different density.
MORTON'S KOSHER: 1 Tablespoon = 15 grams
DIAMOND CRYSTAL: 1 Tablespoon = 21 grams

CHAPTER TWO

Teaching Recipes

This book is meant as a teaching resource, so I've tried to sequence it in a way that is most conducive to learning the process. To start with, I've provided a series of introductory recipes. Some are for dry-cured products, and some not, but each highlights an important aspect of the process. Think of these as the example problems in a textbook; even if you don't try out the recipes, I recommend that you read the narrative accompanying each one.

Coppiette

Coppiette means "couples" in Italian, and refers to long, thin slices of salted meat, tied together in pairs to dry. Coppiette originated as a bar snack, using the cheapest meat available, made just salty enough to keep you drinking wine. While this recipe can be made with any meat (horse is traditional), I recommend starting with a boneless pork loin. Also note that, other than the salt quantities, the flavorings in this recipe are entirely up to you. I'm a fan of hot-pepper flakes on everything, and I also like rolling the meat in black pepper before drying.

Salting Method 1

Salting with a Scale and No Additional Liquid.

Using a precise amount of salt based on the weight of the meat is the ideal way to control the saltiness of your final product. This process is sometimes referred to as equilibrium curing, equilibrium salting, or salting by weight, and is the process used in every recipe in this book. The method requires a couple of basic calculations, but it allows you to precisely adjust a recipe to your tastes. To make it a little easier for you, I'm going to use the example of two pounds of pork loin, and do the calculations for you—using more familiar spoon measurements. You should still use your scale but this will give you a sense of the proportions! (The salt volume measurement is based on Morton's Kosher salt.)

INGREDIENTS

2 lbs (907 grams) Pork Loin (weight after trimming)

WEIGHT AS PERCENTAGE OF MEAT WEIGHT

About 2 Tablespoons (27 grams) Salt, or 3%

About 4 Teaspoons (9 grams) Coriander, or 1%

About 4 Teaspoons (9 grams) Fennel, or 1%

About 4 Teaspoons (9 grams) Crushed Red Pepper, or 1%

INSTRUCTIONS

1. Slice the meat into ¾-inch strips that are at least 8 inches long. Trim off any fat or connective tissue.

2. Weigh the meat, and calculate the quantity of other ingredients based on that weight.

3. Rub the salt and other ingredients into the meat, then place all the meat and any extra salt mixture into a plastic bag in the fridge. Turn occasionally to make sure the salt is evenly distributed, and leave the salted meat in the fridge for at least 3 days. As a result of using a precise quantity of salt based on the weight of the meat, oversalting is not a risk, regardless of how long you leave the meat in the bag.

4. Remove the meat. Tie together two pieces with butcher's twine—side by side so the result resembles a wishbone. These pieces would traditionally be hung over a string or wire in front of a fireplace, but we hang ours in the kitchen from a ceiling beam. In about 72 hours, they will be dry enough to eat. In the middle of a hot and humid summer, you may want to put the slices on a plate in the fridge to dry—just turn them once or twice to make sure they dry evenly.

5. Once the pieces are dry, but before they get tough, store them in a sealed bag or container to prevent overdrying.

WHAT THIS RECIPE TEACHES

Coppiette is true dry-curing: The meat is salted and dried, but never cooked. The final product does not need any refrigeration to be safe to eat, and it will not spoil at room temperature—to use the proper terminology, it is considered shelf-stable at room temperature.

Since this recipe requires an intact piece of meat (as opposed to ground meat), it fits into the whole-muscle dry-curing category. This is one of two types of dry-curing; the other is dry-cured, fermented sausages, such as salami.

All dry-cured meat needs to be salty to help with drying and preservation. The trick is using enough salt to prevent bacteria from growing, but not so much that the meat is inedible. One of the two critical skill sets of dry-curing is the salting process. Making a piece of meat salty is not difficult, and there are multiple approaches to achieving this goal. In this recipe I will outline four different methods for salting; two of them require a scale, two do not.

After salting, the second and final stage of dry-curing whole muscles is the drying stage. The process of drying will be exactly the same regardless of your method of salting. Drying a thin piece of meat like coppiette is easy, but when the meat pieces are larger, drying is the most difficult aspect of dry-curing. Eventually you will want to choose the products you are going to make based on your available drying conditions, keeping in mind that thin cuts of meat are more forgiving than thick ones.

REVIEWING THE MATH YOU NEED

2 pounds pork loin = 907 grams

The amount of salt you want to use is 3% of the total weight of the meat. So 3% = .03 of the meat weight (907 grams) is .03 x 907 = 27.21 grams of salt.

As a point of reference, 15 grams of Morton's kosher salt = 1 tablespoon, so this should be nearly 2 tablespoons. Weigh it! But know that's what it should look like so if it's drastically more or less, check your math.

Salting Method 2

Salting with a Scale in a Brine. Copiette is traditionally salted in a liquid brine, which is unusual for dry-cured meats, but because it was often made from strongly flavored meats, such as horse, it needed the extra flavor and tenderizing that came from red wine. More delicate meats like a pork loin, however, will be overpowered and have a strong wine flavor if they're salted in a red wine brine; white wine or a hard cider may be a better choice for pork loin. This is a good method if you're dry-curing any strongly flavored wild game.

INGREDIENTS

Pork loin

White wine or hard cider (see note), as needed
(you'll need about 2 cups for 2 pounds of pork loin)

WEIGHT AS PERCENTAGE OF MEAT WEIGHT

3% Salt

1% Coriander

1% Fennel

1% Crushed Red Pepper

INSTRUCTIONS

1. Slice the meat into ¾-inch strips that are at least 8 inches long. Trim off any fat or connective tissue. Lay meat in one layer in a tray that you already weighed. Pour over enough wine that pork is fully immersed.

2. Weigh the combined meat and wine (subtracting the weight of the container), and calculate the percentages of salt and other ingredients based on the combined weight of liquid and meat.

3. Place the meat and brine into the fridge and let them sit for at least 48 hours. Since the salt quantity is precisely calculated, the meat cannot become oversalted, so there is no need to worry about leaving the meat for a couple of extra days.

Salting Method 3

Salting with Neither Scale nor Brine.

Without a scale to measure a precise quantity of salt, you must use a method called bulk salting. This involves applying an excess quantity of salt to the meat, whose final saltiness is a direct result of how long you leave it in the salt. To perfect this method, pay attention to how thick your slices of meat are, and keep track of exactly how long the meat sits in the salt. It may take a couple of tries to get the saltiness dialed in to your preference, so you may just want to make a small batch to start. The shape of the meat makes a big difference, but the general rule is 1 day of salting for every kilogram of meat (approximately 1 day of salting for every 2.2 pounds of meat).

In this method, use all the same ingredients as in the above versions, but don't worry about precise quantities. Use enough salt to thickly coat the meat, and mix in the other seasonings in amounts that look good to you. Precision is not important in this recipe; it should be a quick-and-easy process.

INSTRUCTIONS

1. Slice the meat into ¾-inch strips that are at least 8 inches long. Trim off any fat or connective tissue.

2. Mix enough salt to thickly coat the meat with any other seasonings you're using.

3. Coat the meat with a thick layer of the salt/seasoning mixture, set it in a covered container or plastic bag, and put this into the fridge. If the salt didn't coat the meat in a thick layer, add a little more salt over top.

4. Let the meat sit in the salt for 12 to 24 hours.

5. Remove the meat and brush off any extra salt, or rinse it with vinegar or wine. Tie together two pieces with butcher's twine, side-by-side so the result resembles a wishbone. These pieces would traditionally be hung over a string or wire in front of a fireplace, but we hang ours in the kitchen from a ceiling beam. In about 72 hours it's dry enough to eat. In the middle of a hot and humid summer, you may want to put the slices on a plate in the fridge to dry—just turn them once or twice to make sure they dry evenly.

6. Once the pieces are dry, but before they get tough, store them in a sealed bag or container to prevent over-drying.

Salting Method 4
Salting Without a Scale in a Brine. This method is imprecise; it requires you to use some common sense and trial and error, and will not be used in any other recipe in this book. Follow the basic process outlined above, but salt the meat in a brine of wine or hard cider. For every cup of wine, use at least ½ tablespoon of kosher salt, and an amount of seasonings that looks good to you. Leave the meat in the brine for at least 24 hours, and then dry as described above. Expect to adjust this recipe to your own tastes.

Pancetta

Pancetta is dry-cured pork belly, which is the same cut that bacon is made from. Pancetta is a perfect beginner's recipe. It's also aesthetically pleasing and adds great flavor to anything you're cooking, from pasta, to pizza, to a big pot of soup. By far the trickiest part of making pancetta is finding a piece of belly. I've included the volume measurements just to give you a sense of proportions, but remember that any Cure should be measured by weight. Don't use the optional Cure #1 here if you're not using a scale.

WHAT THIS RECIPE TEACHES

Pancetta is another example of true dry-curing. The meat is first salted and then dried, resulting in a product that is shelf-stable.

This recipe uses the technique of salting by weight, and requires some basic math skills and a scale. Every dry-cured recipe from this point on uses the salting-by-weight method.

Salting by weight gives you precise control of the salt concentration in your dry-curing. By measuring salt as a percent of the meat's weight (2.6 to 3.5 percent of it), and allowing enough time for all of the salt to be absorbed and evenly distributed, you remove any risk of over- or undersalting.

This recipe also introduces the need to add curing salt, called Cure #1 (or pink salt), in order to prevent any threat of botulism, but only if you choose to roll your pancetta into the traditional spiral shape. The interior of a rolled pancetta will be an oxygen-free space, and the bacteria that cause botulism produce their toxin only in oxygen-free spaces. Fortunately, curing salts are 100 percent effective in preventing botulism.

Curing salts contain nitrites, and nitrites scare people. This fear is unfounded. It pertains to compounds that form if you burn your meat. Cook the pancetta slowly and you can avoid the issue. More detail on curing salts can be found on page 22. Do not use products such as Morton Sugar Cure in place of curing salt.

INGREDIENTS

5 lbs (2,268 grams) Pork belly

WEIGHT AS PERCENTAGE OF MEAT WEIGHT

About 4.5 Tablespoons (62 grams) Salt, or 2.75%

5.6 grams, or 0.25% Cure #1 (optional)

About 2 Tablespoons (11.3 grams), Black Pepper (toasted and ground), or 0.5%

About 1 Tablespoon (5.6 grams) White Pepper, or 0.25%

About 1 Tablespoon (5.6 grams) Juniper Berries, or 0.25%

About 1 Tablespoon (5.6 grams) Garlic Powder, or 0.25%

About 1 Tablespoon (5.6 grams) Rosemary, or 0.25%

3 Bay Leaves, crumbled

INSTRUCTIONS

1. Trim the edges of the belly to create a uniform rectangle. You can either remove the skin now, or remove it before eating; I prefer to do it now.

2. Weigh the belly, and calculate the quantities of ingredients you'll need using the above percentages.

3. Mix the seasonings, and pack them around the belly. If you plan to roll the belly, be sure to add the optional Cure #1. Place the belly into a plastic bag, and put this into the fridge.

4. Let the belly cure in the fridge for at least a week. During this time, flip the bag occasionally, and make sure the cure is evenly distributed.

5. After at least a week, remove the belly from the bag, rinse, and dry.

6. After salting, but before drying, you can either roll the belly up into a spiral shape, or leave it flat. If you're rolling, cut the skin off and compress the belly into the tightest roll possible. Ideally with someone helping you, tie butcher's twine around the roll to hold its shape. It's important to have no air pockets inside the rolled belly. Tie a loop of butcher's twine to hang the whole roll from.

7. If you're leaving the belly flat, poke two holes in each corner and string butcher's twine through them. Tie each of these into a loop that you can hang the belly from.

8. Hang the belly to dry. You can start cooking with it immediately, but giving it a couple of weeks to dry will concentrate the flavors. I've cured whole flat pieces of belly, carving off slices over an entire year—by the end of a year the flavors had developed into a rich and pungent combination. Pancetta is safe to eat without cooking.

9. Pancetta is often cut into matchstick-sized pieces called lardons and used in a wide variety of dishes. When cooking, brown the pieces over low heat, add any onion or garlic you're using, and proceed with your recipe as usual.

Bacon

Bacon is not a dry-cured product, but it is a cured meat. I include it because bacon is delicious, but it also demonstrates one of the differences between cured meat and dry-cured meat. Bacon is not dried, and as a result, the difficult aspect of making bacon is the hot-smoking—if you're good at smoking meat, bacon is easy.

INGREDIENTS

Pork belly

WEIGHT AS PERCENTAGE OF MEAT WEIGHT

2.25% Salt
0.25% Cure #1 (pink salt)
2%   Maple Syrup
1%   Black Pepper

INSTRUCTIONS

1. Square off the edges of the bacon, creating a uniform rectangle. Leave the skin on if possible, but don't worry if it's already removed. Weigh the trimmed belly.

2. Calculate the amounts of ingredients needed. The amounts of maple syrup and black pepper are flexible, but precision is important when weighing the salt and curing salt. If you'd like more or less salty bacon, adjust the salt percentage as needed, but do not adjust the curing salt amount.

3. Measure the ingredients, and mix them together.

4. Smear the syrupy mixture all over the belly. Place it into a sealed plastic bag, or a vacuum-sealed bag.

5. Put the bag in the fridge and allow it to cure for a week. Turn the bacon occasionally, and make sure the cure is evenly distributed in the bag. Because the quantities are measured by percentage, the meat will not be oversalted if you leave it for too long.

6. After at least a week, remove the bacon, rinse, and then hot-smoke until the internal temperature is 145°F. This will ideally take at least a couple of hours.

7. When the bacon is still hot, remove the skin. Also, sample a thin slice while it's still hot—it's one of the finest tastes of pork you'll have all year.

8. Once it's cool, you can slice it if you want, but I freeze bacon in blocks, cutting slices as needed. When you cook this bacon, use a low heat, as the syrup will burn if you're not careful.

WHAT THIS RECIPE TEACHES

Bacon is cured in salt for a week or two, just like pancetta, but it isn't dried. For this reason, bacon must be refrigerated and needs to be cooked before eating.

You'll occasionally see recipes for dry-cured bacon. This is a different use of the term, and refers to bacon that has had a dry rub applied, as opposed to being cured in a liquid brine (which is common in bacon production). Most dry-cured bacon recipes are probably not true dry-curing, since the meat is never dried.

Another difference between cured meats and dry-cured meats is in the smoking process. Bacon is hot-smoked, and like most commonly smoked meats (ribs, brisket, et cetera), the smoke cooks the bacon.

Dry-cured meats are never cooked, so they cannot be smoked in the same way as bacon. If you want to smoke your dry-curing (which is delicious), use a cold-smoking technique, and the smoke must stay below 90°F. More detail on this on page 29.

Finally, bacon brings back the issue of curing salt. There are two reasons curing salt is used in bacon.

The first is that anytime you smoke meat, either hot-smoke or cold-smoke, there are certain food safety risks. Specifically, you risk creating oxygen-free conditions that may increase the risk of botulism. These risks can be avoided through certain precautions, such as adding curing salt.

The second reason is that the flavor we associate with bacon occurs because of the reactions between the nitrite in the curing salt, and the meat. Nitrite creates the red color of bacon (and ham), and it gives the typical bacon (or ham) flavor. Without nitrite, bacon would not taste like bacon, and ham would just be another piece of roasted pork.

Dry-Cured Tenderloin

Pork tenderloin is easily available and easily dried, and is therefore the perfect meat to practice with, experimenting with different salt levels, techniques, and combinations of flavorings. Dry-cured tenderloin is very lean, so it will not develop the complexity of flavors associated with other cuts of meat.

INGREDIENTS

Pork tenderloin

WEIGHT AS PERCENTAGE OF MEAT WEIGHT

3%	Salt
0.25%	Cure #1 (or Cure #2)
0.5%	Black Pepper
0.5%	Garlic Powder

INSTRUCTIONS

1. Trim the meat into a boneless, cylindrical shape. Make sure there are no cuts in the meat where bacteria could enter, and cut off any stray pieces.

2. Weigh the meat in grams. Write down the weight, then calculate how much of each ingredient you will need. Double-check your math, and measure all the ingredients.

3. Mix the salt and seasonings together, and pack them around the meat. Place the meat and all the extra salt and seasonings in a bag, trying to keep the seasonings as closely in contact with the meat as possible (a vacuum-sealed bag works well).

4. Place the bag in the fridge for at least 2 weeks. Rotate the bag occasionally.

5. After at least 2 weeks has passed, remove the meat from the bag, rinse, and trim again if needed.

6. Dry the meat. Prepare it for hanging by either casing and trussing (page 36), or just trussing it like a roast (page 38). If you are casing the meat, poke lots of holes in the casing with a sausage poker or sterilized needle.

7. Weigh the meat, write the weight on a tag, and attach the tag to the meat.

8. Hang the meat in a dark place, as close to 55°F and 75 percent humidity as possible, but tenderloin is forgiving of variations in temperature and humidity. The meat will need at least two weeks to dry, but check on it frequently, and look for mold growth.

9. When the meat has lost at least 30 percent of its original weight, it's ready to eat. If you used it, remove the casing and slice as thinly as possible.

WHAT THIS RECIPE TEACHES

This recipe is dry-cured, as it is uncooked, salted, and dried. It's shelf-stable at room temperature, and is preserved without the need for refrigeration.

Dry-cured tenderloin provides a good introduction to the process of casing whole muscles for drying. When possible, the meat is stuffed in large sausage casings; the casings slow drying, which allows time for more flavor development, and prevents the formation of a crust. Casing isn't possible for big, flat pieces of pork, like belly, but for cylindrical cuts of meat it's well worth the extra effort.

A wide range of casing is available, in different materials and sizes. Pork tenderloin is probably thin enough to be cased in a standard sausage-sized casing. Casing is not required, and you'll make a great product without it, but it gives you the best results.

Always remove the casing from anything dry-cured, even salami, before eating. For more information about casing, see page 36.

Tenderloin dries easily in most conditions, but as you move into larger cuts of meat, the ideal conditions are 55°F and 75 percent relative humidity. You'll see these same numbers repeated for every recipe.

This recipe also introduces the technique of determining when the meat is ready to eat by calculating the amount of weight the dry meat has lost. If you let the meat dry too much, it will become hard, and the quality quickly deteriorates. This is especially true with a lean cut like tenderloin (which is why I didn't mention these guidelines in the pancetta recipe).

To tell whether the meat is ready to eat, you're looking for a 30 percent weight loss, or for 70 percent of the original weight to remain. Determining this requires weighing before you hang the meat to dry, and re-weighing when you think it's getting close to being ready. The calculation is simple: Divide the final weight by the initial weight, and then multiply by 100 to get the percentage of the weight that remains. Again, you are looking for this number to be around 70 percent, showing a 30 percent weight loss.

You may get your first introduction to mold on your tenderloin. Wipe it off with a vinegar-soaked towel, and don't worry about it.

Finally, this recipe also uses the same curing salt as the previous recipes—often called Cure #1 or pink salt. However, the recipe could be made with a type of curing salt commonly called Cure #2. Cure #2 contains sodium nitrate as well as sodium nitrite, and it's necessary in items that will dry for long periods of time. Tenderloin dries quickly, so Cure #2 is only necessary if you plan to age the meat for longer than two weeks.

Jambons de Camont

This is a recipe passed on to me by Camas Davis of the Portland Meat Collective and is courtesy of her mentors, Dominique Chapolard and Kate Hill. It's a French recipe for curing, cold-smoking, and drying the individual muscle groups that make up a ham. You'll end up with several small "footballs" of smoked and dry-cured ham, which are similar—but superior—to the sliced ham you'd buy in a supermarket deli. Slice thinly and this makes an excellent sandwich filling. This recipe exposes you to some of the many variations you'll come across in recipes found outside of this book. Due to the long and varied history of dry-curing, most recipes you find from other sources will not follow the exact same process of this book, but they all accomplish the same basic goals.

This recipe makes anywhere from 6 to 12 jambons, depending on the size of the ham. The scrap and trim make a wonderful fresh sausage or salami. Trim the skin into long rectangles, scraping away the fat. Roll up and truss—a wonderful addition to beans or soup. The bones will add flavor and body to your soup pot or, once roasted, to a big pot of Italian "gravy."

WHAT THIS RECIPE TEACHES

I've included this recipe as a way to get some low-stress butchering and knife-handling practice, and to expose you to a European style of meat cutting.

When cutting meat for this recipe, or for any dry-curing, you need to forget the standard supermarket treatment of meat and resist chopping the ham into uniform rectangles with a band saw. The traditional cuts of pork used in dry-curing are simply the largest muscle groups from each primal cut of the pig. With some practice, you'll get used to looking for the natural seams between muscles.

The process is a European style of butchery called seam butchery, and the idea is to break a ham into its individual muscle groups—of which there are several. These may range from the size of a grapefruit to that of a football—depending on the starting size of the ham. The individual muscle groups will be obvious once you start cutting.

To begin you'll need a raw, uncured ham, without the skin (you can figure out how to cut the skin off—it doesn't need to be perfect). To begin cutting, just find a seam between two muscle groups. It doesn't matter which seam, because you're going to eventually dismantle the whole ham. Seams are identified by lines where two muscles meet—you might notice a thin white line, or a point where the grain of the meat changes directions, or even a difference in color between two muscle groups. Once you've identified where two muscles meet, use the tip of a sharp knife to slowly separate them. It'll take a little practice, but you'll quickly figure it out. Once you get started, other seams will appear, and it will be obvious how to continue.

You'll end up with several mini hams, and if you make any mistakes, the meat is lean and you can cook it using any roast pork recipe, or fry it up in a pan. Also, while this recipe does not describe the process, each of these mini hams will dry-cure beautifully, using any recipe in this book.

INGREDIENTS

1 fresh, bone-in pork leg

Plenty of coarse Sea Salt

Plenty of coarse-ground Black Pepper

Twine

Compression netting (nice, but not critical)

INSTRUCTIONS

1. Skin the ham and debone.

2. Take out the aitchbone and the leg bone. Follow the seams between each muscle group to carve out the top round, bottom round, eye of round, and knuckle. Clean up each whole muscle by denuding (trimming) the silver skin and any loose bits of fat. Carve these cleaned, larger muscles into small 2- to 3-pound muscles, cutting with the grain and not across it. Carve as many jambons from a whole fresh ham as possible; the yield will range from 6 to 12, depending on the size of the ham. Trim carefully. The more uniform they are, the more evenly they will cure.

3. Rub coarse sea salt into the meat on all sides and into any knife cuts—a scant tablespoon per pound of meat.

4. Refrigerate the jambons, uncovered, on a rack sitting over a sheet pan, for 48 hours.

5. Knock off any remaining salt crystals (most will have been absorbed) and then roll the jambons in a lot—*really a lot*—of cracked black pepper, covering every inch.

6. Half-hitch each jambon into a tight form, then snuggle it inside some elastic netting. (Your butcher might be willing to sell you a couple of feet.)

7. Cold-smoke the jambons for 10 to 12 hours. Hang for about 3 weeks in the proper drying environment or until the jambons have lost 30 percent of their weight.

9. Slice thin and serve.

Carnitas

When all else fails, make carnitas. Carnitas, the ultimate taco filling, is pork confit that is then fried until crispy on the outside, but moist inside. If you're not familiar with the wonders of confit, it's a process of slow-cooking anything submerged in lard. It's not as bad for you as it sounds, as meat isn't a sponge that soaks up fat. The fat simply stops any moisture from exiting the meat. I love dry-cured meat, but carnitas may be my favorite food of all time.

This recipe is crafted for maximum versatility: You can make it with any fatty/tendon/ligament/weird cut of pork that you don't know what to do with. We use this as our universal recipe for pork scraps. We usually save all our scraps and once or twice a year make this recipe, submerge the prepared carnitas in lard, and freeze batches in old yogurt containers.

INGREDIENTS

Enough lard to cover the pork (render your own—it's easy)

Fatty, random scraps of pork

Salt

INSTRUCTIONS

1. The key to this recipe is fat. You want enough lard to submerge all the chunks of meat. Keeping a large quantity of lard in your house may seem absurd, but it's worth it, and you can just freeze it in between uses. Always keep all your scraps of pork fat, and when you have enough, render them into lard (see the note at the end of this recipe for rendering lard).

2. Melt the lard in a slow cooker or big pot.

3. Chunk up any big pieces of pork so they'll lie flat in the slow cooker. Don't worry about trimming out anything—it'll all be easy to remove in a few hours.

4. Put all the pork fully submerged in lard in the slow cooker or pot and set it on low heat.

5. You want the pork to eventually be sitting in a slowly bubbling lake of lard, so watch the meat until you reach this point. Turn the heat as low as you can to maintain the lowest simmer possible—a bubble every few seconds is ideal.

6. After several hours of cooking, the meat should easily pull apart with a fork—but don't rush it. Once the meat reaches this point, remove it from the lard and allow it to cool.

7. When cool enough to handle, separate the meat from any fat, connective tissue, bones, or anything else that doesn't look appetizing. Keep the meat in pieces as large as possible while doing this.

8. At this point, any meat you aren't going to eat immediately can be placed into a leftovers container, covered with the still-liquid lard, left to cool and harden, and then placed in the freezer. It will last for months in this condition.

9. For any meat you are eating now, break the meat into baseball-sized pieces (if they're already smaller, no problem). Put the pieces into a deep, hot skillet with a couple of tablespoons of hot lard. The meat won't need much lard to fry nicely, and the fat may splatter, so be ready to contain any mess.

10. Fry the meat until it's crispy. If you're making a lot of carnitas, you can do this under a broiler on a roasting pan. If you use the broiler, turn the meat every 5 minutes or so to obtain even browning.

11. Once the meat is browned and crispy, remove it from the skillet, salt it generously, and serve it with warm corn tortillas, a squeeze of lime, and your favorite hot sauce.

WHAT THIS RECIPE TEACHES

Perhaps the most important lesson of all: Never throw out any raw pork. It can always be turned into carnitas.

Also, sometimes when all the measuring and precision of dry-curing is too much, you just need to wing it and use some common sense. That's the best attitude to approach this recipe with.

NOTE

To render lard, you need a bunch of fat—if you make a lot at once, you won't need to do it again for a while. We make about 5 pounds at a time. Ideally you can use fatback or the fat surrounding the kidney (leaf lard); the latter has the cleanest flavor, though this is only important if you're making pastries or piecrust. Chop the fat into small pieces, or run it through your grinder. Place all the fat into a big pot (or a slow cooker—the ideal choice) with a little water at the bottom, and cook slowly until the fat starts to melt. Keep it at a low simmer until everything is melted, strain off the liquid from the leftover scraps (cracklings), let it cool, and you've got lard. You may want to pull the liquid off with a ladle as it melts—this can speed up the process.

CHAPTER THREE

Whole-Muscle Dry-Curing

Whole-muscle dry-curing is the simplest of all dry-curing, as it simply involves salting a piece of meat, then hanging it to dry. That being said, the umbrella of whole-muscle dry-curing contains the finest dry-cured meats in the world. This simple process can keep you occupied for a lifetime.

Examples of whole-muscle dry-curing include pancetta, coppa (capicola), guanciale, culatello, and speck. Each of these products is made from a specific cut of pork, but you can dry-cure any cut of meat, such as braesola, made from beef, or even duck breast. Bone-in dry-cured hams, such as prosciutto di Parma and jamon, also technically fall into this category, but require a more involved process. To avoid confusion, dry-cured hams have a dedicated chapter later on in the book.

Dry-curing a whole muscle is an excellent place to begin dry-curing. It is much simpler than making salami, requires less stringent environmental control than a ham, and tastes and looks amazing. Additionally, a good piece of meat is relatively sterile inside, making it easier to control unwanted microorganisms than in a salami. Dry-curing a thin cut of pork, such as a pancetta or tenderloin, is a simple and quick introduction to the process.

Meat

In its best and most basic form, whole-muscle dry-curing is a showcase for the flavors and complexities of a good piece of meat. The characteristics of the pig's diet, breed, and home are accentuated with a little salt, and the flavors are concentrated by the evaporation of water from the meat. If you have a source for interesting pork and want to taste it in its most pure form, there is no better way than dry-curing with a simple recipe of salt, curing salt, and maybe a little freshly cracked pepper.

Every muscle group of the pig can be salted and dried using the exact same process, with the exception being the ham, which requires special treatment only because of its large size and the bone (but which still generally follows the same process). For this reason, don't let your lack of access to an authentic Italian butcher stop you; use whatever boneless cuts of pork you can get your hands on.

As you get started, focus on cuts of pork that are easy to source. Boneless loin and tenderloin can be found almost anywhere; belly is another good option but can be a little harder to find. Remember, every part of a pig can be dry-cured, and if you're not sure you have the perfect coppa, as long as it's a solid piece of pork without any cuts, nicks, or flaps, dry-cure it.

SOURCING THE RIGHT CUTS FOR DRY-CURING

Italians butcher their pigs in a way that optimizes the meat for dry-curing, in contrast with American butchers, who optimize for pork chops and bacon. This difference results in Italian cuts of pork and American cuts of pork not matching up perfectly. If this concerns you, start a relationship with a good butcher, and talk with them about what you're trying to achieve.

Any attempt to summarize the wide range of dry-cure products will have its flaws and omissions, but the following is a general description of muscle groups and their corresponding Italian, dry-cured names.

BACK LEG/HAM

Prosciutto Crudo/Jamon

The whole bone-in, skin-on ham, salted, dried, and aged. The large size and bone require you to take a different approach to dry-curing than other cuts, and the detailed description of the process begins on page 84. The term *prosciutto* is commonly used to describe dry-cured hams, but it's a general term; *prosciutto cotto* is a cooked ham, and *prosciutto crudo* a dry-cured, uncooked ham (including prosciutto di Parma). *Prosciutto crudo* is the Italian version, and *jamon* is the Spanish version of a dry-cured ham. A properly aged prosciutto and jamon are among the finest foods in the world.

Culatello and Fiocco

If you picture a ham still attached to the pig, the culatello is the big muscle group behind the thighbone, and the fiocco is the small muscle group in front of that bone, sometimes called the knuckle. These require deboning the ham, and are a good alternative to dry-curing a bone-in ham, as they are much easier to salt and don't require the skin to be left on. The culatello is considered by some to be superior to the best prosciutto or jamon.

Speck

Speck refers to a wide range of products, one of which is a deboned and butterflied ham that is cured, cold-smoked, and then dried. The result is a large, flat oval of meat.

LOIN

Coppiette

Kind of like Italian jerky. The perfect beginner's recipe, this traditional Italian snack is uncommon in the United States. It's simply long, thin strips of loin or tenderloin, salted and dried. The thin strips allow drying to happen quickly, so no special conditions are needed, as long as you avoid excess heat or humidity. Historically these are made with horse meat and other animals.

Lonza/Lonzino/Lomo

Dry-cured boneless pork loin. Perhaps the easiest raw cut to find, and relatively easy to dry, the loin is another great recipe for beginners and intermediates.

This is a lean cut, so it's good for those who haven't yet embraced the beauty of dry-cured fat.

FATBACK

Lardo

This is made from the fat that runs under the skin, around and above the spine of the pig. Lardo is pure fat, and while delicious it's definitely not for everyone. The breed and diet of the pig will heavily influence the thickness, texture, and overall quality of the fat.

TENDERLOIN

When dry-cured, Jacques Pepin calls this saucisson of tenderloin; Ruhlman and Polcyn call it filetto in their book *Salumi*. The tenderloin is not commonly dry-cured, as it is a great cooked meal, especially on butchering day. Regardless, dry-cured tenderloin is tasty, simple, a quick project, and a good place to start dry-curing or to test new flavor combinations. Dry-cured tenderloin is lean and lacks the flavor and fattiness of other cuts, but it absorbs flavor well.

BELLY

Pancetta

This is the exact same cut used to make bacon. Indeed, pancetta is similar to bacon, except it's not hot-smoked, as bacon is, and bacon isn't dried, the way pancetta is. Pancetta is another easy place to begin your dry-curing, as the thin shape of a the belly makes drying almost foolproof, and a little pancetta makes everything taste better. Pancetta is most often sold rolled into a spiral, but rolling isn't necessary, or even traditional in many areas.

Dry-Cured Bacon

This terminology can get confusing, since in the United States dry-cured bacon might refer to the curing agent (salt and nitrites) being dry (applied as a rub), as opposed to curing with a water-based brine. Ignoring this confusion, you can create a true dry-cured bacon, which can be eaten raw, by cold-smoking and drying a salted belly. Basically it's just a cold-smoked pancetta.

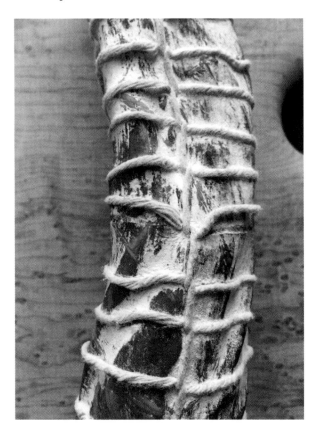

NECK/SHOULDER/BOSTON BUTT

Coppa/Capocollo/Cappicola/Gabagoul

One of the prizes of a pig, the coppa is a beautifully marbled, flavorful piece of meat. To identify the coppa, imagine patting a pig on the back of its neck; the two coppa are just under your hand, on each side of the spine. For more detail, if you follow the loin toward the head of the pig, it transitions into the coppa in the neck area. There is no distinct separation from the coppa and loin, just a transition from the lean, tender meat of the loin into the fatty, tougher meat of the coppa. It is difficult to source a whole coppa in the United States, because in the process of maximizing the number of pork chops you get from a pig, you lose the back end of the coppa. Don't worry about this—a short coppa dry-cures just as nicely as a long coppa. To source a coppa, buy a Boston butt and cut away the flaps to isolate the largest uniform cylinder of meat, which is primarily the coppa.

SHOULDER/FRONT LEG

Speck/Spalla Speck

This is a skin-on, deboned, and butterflied front leg/shoulder that is cold-smoked and dried. The final product is a flattened oval. This might be the greatest pizza topping of all time.

Prosciutto

Simply put, a prosciutto made with the front leg. Similar to but different from a standard prosciutto.

JOWL
Guanciale
The skin-on cheek muscle of a pig. The jowl is fatty, flavorful, and tough. Dry-curing it results in a product similar to pancetta that, like pancetta, can be used in a wide range of cooking. If you can get a jowl, it is easy to dry-cure. This is a classic ingredient in pasta carbonara.

OTHER TYPES OF MEAT
While pork is the focus of most dry-curing in this country, and this book, whether for religious reasons, preference, or availability, goat, beef, duck, and horse meat are all commonly dry-cured. For example, a goat leg is a great place to begin experimenting with bone-in cuts, as it's small enough to easily absorb the cure and dries quickly. Don't limit yourself to pork. Follow these same basic steps, and you'll be successful with most types of meat.

Salt

The goal when salting a whole muscle is an even distribution of a precise amount of salt throughout the meat. There are several ways of accomplishing this. As noted in the introductory recipes, I focus on a simple technique called salting by weight or equilibrium curing. This method involves putting a precise amount of salt, the meat, and any other desired seasonings into a closed plastic bag, and waiting a couple of weeks for it all to equilibrate. With the exception of bone-in hams, all whole muscles can be salted in this same, simple way.

Another technique, called bulk salting, can be used, but I don't recommend it. In this process, the meat is salted by rubbing an excess quantity of salt onto it or even burying it in salt, and letting the salt absorb over several days, with the length of time determining the final saltiness. Because of its speed and simplicity, bulk salting is commonly used in commercial production. Commercial producers have an advantage over home producers in the bulk salting process: They are making the same thing over and over, with the same breeds of pig, being fed the same diet, and being slaughtered at the same age. This gives them the benefit of thousands of trials to refine their process. If you're a home producer making a wide variety of products, using different breeds of pigs, fed different diets, slaughtered at different ages, and butchered in different ways, it is hard to refine your technique for bulk salting. The salting-by-weight technique, however, gives you an exact level of precision and control that will allow you to refine your recipes to your tastes.

Drying and Aging

Before hanging any whole muscle or salami to dry, record the weight and the date, and any notes that will help you identify the specific recipe you used. Attach this information to the meat. This data is critical in determining when the meat is ready to eat, and it's easy to forget the specifics of each cut when they're all hanging side by side.

Additionally, before drying, you may want to inoculate the outside of the meat with a purchased mold culture. While not necessary, a healthy population of good mold can improve the quality of your final product by regulating drying, contributing to the complexity of flavors, and outcompeting undesirable mold. Mold cultures are bought in dehydrated packets. Once you've rehydrated one in distilled water, you can use a spray bottle to inoculate the meat, or dip the meat in the mold culture. For more details on mold, see page 41.

Whether or not you inoculate with a mold culture, as the meat dries—and especially at the beginning when the moisture content is high—regularly check for unwanted mold, and wipe off any you find with a vinegar-soaked towel.

The general criteria are that dry-cured meats are ready to eat after a 30 percent weight loss, and that you want to dry at 55°F and 75 percent relative humidity. The time needed to reach 30 percent weight loss varies, but once you've created some consistency in your products and drying conditions, you'll be able to predict the required time with some accuracy.

While aging can increase the complexity of flavors in your dry-cured meat, don't overdry the meat. The meat is best with some moisture, and overdrying will only result in a salty, hard block of meat.

Whole-Muscle Dry-Curing: The Detailed Process

1. Make your plan for the salting and curing stage: You need meat, a scale, the recipe and ingredients, a sealable plastic bag, and fridge space. Also make sure you have a plan for the upcoming drying stage.

2. Using the highest-quality meat available, trim the meat into a uniform shape. Your goal is an intact piece, without any cuts into the muscle, which could introduce bacteria.

3. Weigh the meat. Use grams as your unit of measure; ounces are not precise enough for ingredients such as curing salt.

4. Based on the weight of the meat, measure out all the ingredients you are using, and mix them together.

5. Pack the meat in an even coating of the salt and seasonings. Put the meat and any remaining salt mixture in a sealable plastic bag (vacuum-sealed bags work great for this).

6. Place the bagged meat in the fridge. Rotate the meat occasionally to assure even distribution of the contents. Leave all exuded liquid in the bag.

7. You now have time to prepare for the drying stage, and time to order any supplies you've realized you don't have. You'll need at minimum a scale, butcher's twine (16-ply cotton), a place to dry the meat, and a thermometer/humidity meter. Eventually, you may also want large casings (big enough to fit around the whole muscle) and mold inoculant.

8. Once the meat/salt mixture has equilibrated, which may take 2 or 3 weeks (but it's impossible for me to tell you an exact time), remove the meat from the bag, rinse it, pat it dry, and do a final trimming of the muscle, finishing with a smooth piece of meat with no gouges or flaps.

9. If you're casing the meat, stuff it in the casing and truss it. If you won't be casing the muscle, just tie the meat so you can hang it (page 38).

10. If you're cold-smoking, do that now. Make sure the temperature doesn't get too warm (page 29).

11. If you're inoculating with mold, do that now. Don't use mold if you've cold-smoked the meat (the smoke will inhibit mold growth) (page 41).

12. Weigh the meat, and record the date and weight on a tag or piece of tape attached to it.

13. Hang the meat to dry. Check on it, daily at first, and pay close attention to the humidity and temperature. Clean off any unwanted mold with a vinegar-soaked towel (page 41).

14. Weigh occasionally. After the meat has lost 30 percent of its weight, it's ready to eat. Remove the casing and slice the meat paper-thin (page 49).

15. If the meat is finished drying before you're ready to eat it, or you're taking your time and savoring it, seal the meat well in a plastic bag (or ideally a vacuum-sealed bag), and freeze.

The Basic Dry-Cured Loin (Lonzino)

Dry-cured loin is a perfect introductory recipe, as it's got a great flavor, is relatively easy to dry, and it doesn't have the high fat content that some people aren't used to. That being said, if you're cutting up a pig and can leave the fatback attached to the loin, you'll get a wonderful combination of lean pork loin, essentially with lardo attached. When you finally get to eat your dry-cured loin, serve it with lemon juice and cracked pepper.

INGREDIENTS

Pork Loin

WEIGHT AS PERCENTAGE OF MEAT WEIGHT

3%	Salt
0.25%	Cure #2
0.5%	Black Pepper

INSTRUCTIONS

1. Trim the meat into a boneless, uniform shape. Make sure there are no cuts in the meat where bacteria could enter, and cut off any stray pieces.

2. Weigh the meat in grams. Write down the weight, then calculate how much of each ingredient you will need. Double-check your math, and measure all the ingredients.

3. Mix all the salt and seasonings together, and pack them around the meat. Place the meat and all the extra salt and seasonings in a bag, trying to keep the seasonings as closely in contact with the meat as possible (a vacuum-sealed bag works well).

4. Place the bag in the fridge for at least 2 weeks. Rotate the bag occasionally.

5. After at least 2 weeks has passed, remove the meat from the bag, rinse, dry, and trim again if needed.

6. Prepare the cured meat for hanging by either casing and trussing (page 37), or just trussing it like a roast (page 38). If you are casing the meat, poke lots of holes in the casing with a sausage poker or sterilized needle. If you're inoculating with mold, do it now.

7. Weigh the meat and write it down on a tag. Attach the tag to the meat.

8. Hang the meat in a dark place that is as close to 55°F and 75 percent humidity as possible. The meat will need at least a month to dry, but check on it frequently, and look for mold growth (which is expected). Remove unwanted mold with a vinegar-soaked towel.

9. When the meat has lost at least 30 percent of its original weight, it is ready to eat. Remove the casing, if used, and slice as thin as possible.

Dry-Cured Loin with Juniper and Garlic

Dry-cured loin accepts flavors well, but be aware that the spices will quickly overwhelm the flavor of the meat. This is a simple recipe, and I really like the juniper's flavor contribution.

INGREDIENTS

Pork Loin

WEIGHT AS PERCENTAGE OF MEAT WEIGHT

3%	Salt
0.25%	Cure #2
1%	Black Pepper
0.10%	Juniper Berries
0.25%	Garlic Powder

INSTRUCTIONS

1. Trim the meat into a boneless, uniform shape. Make sure there are no cuts in the meat where bacteria could enter, and cut off any stray pieces.

2. Weigh the meat in grams. Write down the weight, then calculate how much of each ingredient you will need. Double-check your math, and measure all the ingredients.

3. Mix all the salt and seasonings together, and pack them around the meat. Place the meat and all the extra salt and seasonings in a bag, trying to keep the seasonings as closely in contact with the meat as possible (a vacuum-sealed bag works well).

4. Place the bag in the fridge for at least 2 weeks. Rotate the bag occasionally.

5. After at least 2 weeks has passed, remove the meat from the bag, rinse, dry, and trim again if needed.

6. Prepare it for hanging by either casing and trussing (page 37), or just trussing it like a roast (page 38). If you are casing the meat, poke lots of holes in the casing with a sausage poker or sterilized needle. If you're inoculating with mold, do it now.

7. Weigh the meat and write it down on a tag. Attach the tag to the meat.

8. Hang the meat in a dark place, as close to 55°F and 75 percent humidity as possible. The meat will need at least a month to dry, but check on it frequently, and look for mold growth (which is expected). Remove unwanted mold with a vinegar-soaked towel.

9. When the meat has lost at least 30 percent of its original weight, it is ready to eat. Remove the casing, if used, and slice as thin as possible.

The Basic Guanciale

Guanciale, the skin-on, dry-cured jowl of a pig, is often used in pasta carbonara, but can be used anytime you would use pancetta or bacon. Because it's usually cooked, if you don't plan on aging the guanciale for a long period of time, substitute Cure #1 for Cure #2. Be sure to remove any glands when trimming out your jowl—they'll have a pebbled appearance and simply look different from everything else. You'll get so you easily recognize them, but it might take some time. I find I need to cut away more than I expect when trimming out the glands. Keep trimming until the texture of the meat and fat looks uniform.

This is a simple recipe, but don't hesitate to add fennel, red pepper, juniper, or anything else that sounds good.

INGREDIENTS

Pork Jowl/Cheek

WEIGHT AS PERCENTAGE OF MEAT WEIGHT

3% Salt
0.25% Cure #2
0.5% Black Pepper

INSTRUCTIONS

1. Trim the meat into a boneless, uniform shape. Make sure there are no cuts where bacteria could enter, and cut off any stray pieces.

2. Weigh the meat in grams. Write down the weight, then calculate how much of each ingredient you will need. Double-check your math, and measure all the ingredients.

3. Mix all the salt and seasonings together, and pack them around the meat. Place the meat and all the extra salt and seasonings in a bag, trying to keep the seasonings as closely in contact with the meat as possible (a vacuum-sealed bag works well).

4. Place the bag in the fridge for at least 2 weeks. Rotate the bag occasionally.

5. After at least 2 weeks has passed, remove the meat from the bag, rinse, dry, and trim again if needed.

6. Prepare it for hanging by poking a hole in a corner and tying a loop of twine through.

7. Weigh the meat and write it down on a tag. Attach the tag to the meat.

8. Hang the meat in a dark place, as close to 55°F and 75 percent humidity as possible. The meat will need at least a month to dry, but check on it frequently, and look for mold growth. Remove unwanted mold with a vinegar-soaked towel.

9. When the meat has lost at least 30 percent of its original weight, it is ready to eat.

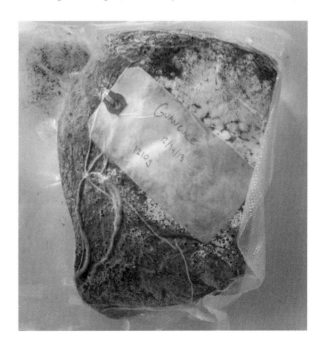

Speck

Like so much of Italian dry-curing terminology, speck refers to a variety of products. Maybe most familiarly, the term refers to a skin-on, deboned, and butterflied ham, salted, cold-smoked, and then dried. The result is a product much more forgiving to produce than a whole bone-in ham. It's a good option if you've got a ham and aren't ready to tackle a prosciutto.

We make our speck out of the front leg of the pig. We leave the skin on, remove the bone, and trim substantially, creating as uniform a thickness as possible.

When you're ready to eat your speck, slice the skin off and cut thinly. If you have a nice fatty pig, the contrast between a thin layer of smoky meat and a rich layer of fat is delicious. We served this at my brother's wedding, and it was the definitely the favorite of all the dry-cured meats.

INGREDIENTS

Deboned and butterflied pork leg—either the front or back leg.

WEIGHT AS PERCENTAGE OF MEAT WEIGHT

3%   Salt
0.25% Cure #2
0.20% Black Pepper
0.20% Juniper Berries
0.20% Garlic Powder
0.20% Rosemary
0.10% Bay Leaf
0.10% Thyme
0.10% Sage

INSTRUCTIONS

1. Debone the ham or picnic ham, and then trim the meat into a boneless, uniform shape. Make sure there are no cuts where bacteria could enter, and cut off any stray pieces.

2. Weigh the meat in grams. Write down the weight, then calculate how much of each ingredient you will need. Double-check your math, and measure all the ingredients.

3. Mix all the salt and seasonings together, and pack them around the meat. Place the meat and all the extra salt and seasonings in a bag, trying to keep the seasonings as closely in contact with the meat as possible (a vacuum-sealed bag works well).

4. Place the bag in the fridge for at least 2 weeks. Rotate the bag occasionally.

5. After at least 2 weeks has passed, remove the meat from the bag, rinse, dry, and trim again if needed. Thread a couple of loops of twine through two corners.

6. Cold-smoke the meat for at least 2 days.

7. Weigh the meat and write it down on a tag. Attach the tag to the meat.

8. Hang the meat in a dark place, as close to 55°F and 75 percent humidity as possible. The meat will need at least a month to dry, but check on it frequently, and look for mold growth. Remove unwanted mold with a vinegar-soaked towel.

9. When the meat has lost at least 30 percent of its original weight, it is ready to eat.

The Basic Coppa

One of the best parts of a pig, a nice coppa will have a beautiful marbling of lean meat and fat. This recipe is kept simple to show off the flavors of the meat, but add any seasoning to this recipe—just remember to write down what you used, and how much, for future reference. Coppa is another product that is best served with just squeezed lemon and cracked pepper.

INGREDIENTS

Pork Shoulder/Neck

WEIGHT AS PERCENTAGE OF MEAT WEIGHT

3%	Salt
0.25%	Cure #2
0.5%	Black Pepper

INSTRUCTIONS

1. Trim the meat into a boneless, uniform shape. Make sure there are no cuts in the meat where bacteria could enter, and cut off any stray pieces.

2. Weigh the meat in grams. Write down the weight, then calculate how much of each ingredient you will need. Double-check your math, and measure all the ingredients.

3. Mix all the salt and seasonings together, and pack them around the meat. Place the meat and all the extra salt and seasonings in a bag, trying to keep the seasonings as closely in contact with the meat as possible (a vacuum-sealed bag works well).

4. Place the bag in the fridge for at least 2 weeks. Rotate the bag occasionally.

5. After at least 2 weeks has passed, remove the meat from the bag, rinse, dry, and trim again if needed.

6. Prepare it for hanging by either casing and trussing (page 37), or just trussing it like a roast (page 38). If you are casing the meat, poke lots of holes in the casing with a sausage poker or sterilized needle.

7. Weigh the meat and write it down on a tag. Attach the tag to the meat.

8. Hang the meat in a dark place that is as close to 55°F and 75 percent humidity as possible. The meat will need at least a month to dry, but check on it frequently, and look for mold growth. Remove unwanted mold with a vinegar-soaked towel.

9. When the meat has lost at least 30 percent of its original weight, it is ready to eat. Remove the casing, if used, and slice as thin as possible.

Smoked Spicy Coppa

This recipe may be the biggest crowd pleaser of all. Its smoky spiciness seems to hit American palates just right (including mine). Remember to only cold-smoke; in this case, you can do it for several days and it still won't be overpowering. Also, feel free to use as much hot pepper as you can. I've never made a too-spicy coppa, no matter how much hot pepper I added.

If you're trying to get a really spicy product, you can coat the coppa in chili powder before you case it—but it's somewhat counterproductive, as you'll lose most of the chili powder when you force the meat into the casing. You can also try hot pepper flakes, which may stick better—or, if you're feeling motivated, cut the casing, place the powdered coppa in the casing, and sew it back up using any needle and thread.

INGREDIENTS

Pork Shoulder/Neck

WEIGHT AS PERCENTAGE OF MEAT WEIGHT

3%	Salt
0.25%	Cure #2
0.5%	Black Pepper
0.20%	White Pepper
2%	Hot Red Chili Powder
0.5%	Garlic Powder

INSTRUCTIONS

1. Trim the meat into a boneless, uniform shape. Make sure there are no cuts in the meat where bacteria could enter, and cut off any stray pieces.

2. Weigh the meat in grams. Write down the weight, then calculate how much of each ingredient you will need. Double-check your math, and measure all the ingredients.

3. Mix all the salt and seasonings together, and pack them around the meat. Place the meat and all the extra salt and seasonings in a bag, trying to keep the seasonings as closely in contact with the meat as possible (a vacuum-sealed bag works well).

4. Place the bag in the fridge for at least 2 weeks. Rotate the bag occasionally.

5. After at least 2 weeks has passed, remove the meat from the bag, rinse, dry, and trim again if needed.

6. Prepare it for hanging by either casing and trussing (page 37), or just trussing it like a roast (page 38). If you are casing the meat, poke lots of holes in the casing with a sausage poker or sterilized needle.

7. Before hanging the meat to dry, cold-smoke for at least 2 days.

8. Weigh the meat and write it down on a tag. Attach the tag to the meat.

9. Hang the meat in a dark place that is as close to 55°F and 75 percent humidity as possible. The meat will need at least a month to dry, but check on it frequently, and look for mold growth. Remove unwanted mold with a vinegar-soaked towel.

10. When the meat has lost at least 30 percent of its original weight, it is ready to eat. Remove the casing, if used, and slice as thin as possible.

Fiocco

Fiocco is traditionally made from what is sometimes referred to as the "shin" meat of the back leg. It's what's left over when you trim out a culatello, but if you want to practice cutting up a ham into its individual muscle groups (page 80), this recipe can be used to dry-cure any of the components that make up a ham.

INGREDIENTS

Small "football" shaped piece of a deboned ham

WEIGHT AS PERCENTAGE OF MEAT WEIGHT

3%	Salt
0.25%	Cure #2
0.25%	Black Pepper

INSTRUCTIONS

1. Trim the meat into a boneless, uniform shape. Make sure there are no cuts where bacteria could enter, and cut off any stray pieces.

2. Weigh the meat in grams. Write down the weight, then calculate how much of each ingredient you will need. Double-check your math, and measure all the ingredients.

3. Mix all the salt and seasonings together, and pack them around the meat. Place the meat and all the extra salt and seasonings in a bag, trying to keep the seasonings as closely in contact with the meat as possible (a vacuum-sealed bag works well).

4. Place the bag in the fridge for at least 2 weeks. Rotate the bag occasionally.

5. After at least 2 weeks has passed, remove the meat from the bag, rinse, dry, and trim again if needed.

6. Prepare it for hanging by either casing it in a beef bung and trussing or just trussing it like a roast. If you are casing the meat, poke lots of holes in the casing with a sausage poker or sterilized needle.

7. Weigh the meat and write it down on a tag. Attach the tag to the meat.

8. Hang the meat in a dark place, as close to 55°F and 75 percent humidity as possible. The meat will need at least a month to dry, but check on it frequently, and look for mold growth. Remove unwanted mold with a vinegar-soaked towel.

9. When the meat has lost at least 30 percent of its original weight, it is ready to eat. Remove the casing, if used, and slice as thin as possible.

Culatello

Made from the biggest boneless muscle mass in the back leg, the culatello is considered by many to be the finest dry-cured product of all. That being said, deboning a ham doesn't suddenly make it the best—it's your raw product, process, and environment that will determine if your culatello is world-class.

Culatello is basically the muscle mass behind the back leg—comparable to the thigh muscle. If you're looking at the leg from the side of a pig, the muscle on the front side of the back leg is the fiocco, and the muscle mass on the back side of the leg is the culatello. Debone the ham from the side, isolating the front and back muscle masses. Consult the fiocco recipe for the front, and this recipe for the big piece.

Culatello is traditionally cased in a beef bladder. This is sliced open, the culatello is placed inside, and the bladder is sewn back up. Beef bladders are difficult to source but are available with some searching.

INGREDIENTS

The largest intact piece of a deboned ham

WEIGHT AS PERCENTAGE OF MEAT WEIGHT

3%	Salt
0.25%	Cure #2
0.5%	Black Pepper

INSTRUCTIONS

1. Trim the meat into a boneless, uniform shape. Make sure there are no cuts where bacteria could enter, and cut off any stray pieces.

2. Weigh the meat in grams. Write down the weight, then calculate how much of each ingredient you will need. Double-check your math, and measure all the ingredients.

3. Mix all the salt and seasonings together, and pack them around the meat. Place the meat and all the extra salt and seasonings in a bag, trying to keep the seasonings as closely in contact with the meat as possible (a vacuum-sealed bag works well).

4. Place the bag in the fridge for at least 2 weeks. Rotate the bag occasionally.

5. After at least 2 weeks has passed, remove the meat from the bag, rinse, dry, and trim again if needed.

6. Prepare it for hanging by either casing it in a beef bung and trussing or just trussing it like a roast. If you are casing the meat, poke lots of holes in the casing with a sausage poker or sterilized needle.

7. Weigh the meat and write it down on a tag. Attach the tag to the meat.

8. Hang the meat in a dark place, as close to 55°F and 75 percent humidity as possible. The meat will need at least a month to dry, but check on it frequently, and look for mold growth. Remove unwanted mold with a vinegar-soaked towel.

9. When the meat has lost at least 30 percent of its original weight, it is ready to eat. Remove the casing, and slice as thin as possible.

Lardo

Lardo is simply cured fat, and the quality of lardo relies almost entirely on the raw product. It's just a slab of fatback, and it may take some searching to find a thick enough (3 inches) piece—I've never found thick enough fatback from a standard butcher, only directly from farms.

Lardo is cured with a different method than other dry-cured meats use. In fact, it isn't actually dry-cured, but we're not going to let that detail get in our way. Lardo is salted, traditionally in marble boxes, and it sits for months in the salt and briny liquid that forms in the containers. I cure lardo in a tightly sealed bag, and since it needs to be cured in a dark space to prevent degradation of the fat, I wrap the bag in a couple of layers of foil.

Lardo is also sometimes cured in liquid brine, which I haven't experimented with. As with all cured meat preparations, different techniques all can have great results, as long as you take the time to refine your process.

INGREDIENTS

Fatback, ideally two or three inches thick, and
as big a piece as possible.

WEIGHT AS PERCENTAGE OF FAT WEIGHT

3%	Salt
0.25%	Cure #2
1.5%	Black Pepper
0.5%	White Pepper
0.5%	Rosemary
0.5%	Bay Leaf

INSTRUCTIONS

1. Trim the skin off the fatback and any lean meat that may be attached.

2. Mix the seasonings, pack them onto the fatback, and enclose in a sealed (or vacuum-sealed) bag.

3. Wrap the bag in aluminum foil, to block the light. Fat will react with light.

4. Leave the fat in the bag, in the fridge, for at least 6 months.

5. Remove the fat, slice thin, and eat on a warm piece of bread.

CHAPTER FOUR

Salami

Many people, myself included, become interested in dry-curing in order to make salami. While salami isn't difficult to make, by starting your dry-curing practice with whole muscles, you have a much higher likelihood of success. That being said, if you are experienced at making sausage, and you are confident in your ability to dry a sausage, you can absolutely make a successful salami on your first try, but perfecting the nuances will keep you busy for a long time.

For being the most familiar of all dry-cured meats, most people would have a hard time defining what salami actually is. The technical definition of *salami* is "an uncooked, fermented, and dried sausage." While fermented and dried sausages are found in many cultures, the Italian term *salami* is the simplest word to encompass all these products.

Salami is a type of sausage. There are countless varieties of sausage found around the world; salami is just one. It's saltier than many sausages, because the salt prevents unwanted bacteria from growing, but still allows beneficial bacteria to thrive.

Second, salami is fermented. Fermentation is one of two defining traits of salami, with drying being the other. When preparing salami, you add sugar into the meat mixture, and you add a purchased culture of beneficial bacteria and yeast. The added bacteria consume the sugar, and produce lactic acid as a by-product, which drops the salami's pH (a low pH is more acidic) while also creating many new flavors. Fermentation is important for a couple of reasons. One, by growing a big population of good bacteria, you'll outcompete any bad bacteria; two, the lactic acid produced will either help preserve the meat, or help the meat dry.

If you use a lot of sugar, the bacteria will produce a lot of lactic acid, and the salami gets really sour. In this case the lactic acid helps preserve the meat in the same way that vinegar helps preserve pickles. Alternatively, if you add just a little sugar, only a small amount of acid is produced. This isn't enough to preserve the meat, but the small drop in pH triggers the release of water from the meat's proteins, which promotes drying the meat. Some American salamis are very acidic with a strong tangy flavor, while traditional European-style salamis have a very mild acid profile. Be prepared for fermentation to be an unattractive, smelly, warm, and slimy experience, but consider this a sign that everything is proceeding as planned.

Third, salami must be dried. As with all the meats in this book, drying is critical to preventing bacterial growth and allows salami to be consumed without cooking.

Salami is only one type of fermented sausage, and the only type described in this book, but there are many types of fermented sausages that are never dried. Summer sausage is a good example of a fermented sausage that is cooked instead of dried. Summer sausage is fermented to a low pH (high acid), and then cooked; this combination of an acidic environment and cooking is what allows it to be kept unrefrigerated. The variety of meat sticks you'll find in a gas station are also often fermented and then cooked, which adds to their flavor, and increases their shelf life. Fermentation will naturally begin in any meat that is left to sit at room temperature for a couple of days. The fermentation of meat has been embraced by many cultures in different forms, with salami just being one type.

Starter Cultures and Sugar

The availability of starter cultures for salami fermentation is the reason we can safely make salami at home. Only recently available for the home producer, starter cultures provide a reliable population of beneficial microorganisms, with well-understood characteristics, that will produce a series of desireable results in a fermenting salami.

There are several benefits related to fermenting a salami. The most noticeable is the production of lactic acid, which increases the acidity of the salami (lowering the pH), but fermentation also produces a complex array of flavors, improves color and flavor stability of the salami, and produces a large population of beneficial bacteria, which will outcompete any unwanted bacteria.

There are many types of starter cultures available, each with their own characteristics, and their own carefully crafted combination of microorganisms. When purchasing a starter culture for salami, look for a traditional southern European flavor profile, as there are many different types of meat starter cultures. I recommend choosing starter cultures labeled "Bioprotective," as the microorganisms in this line of cultures have been chosen for their ability to limit the growth of harmful bacteria—listeria being the primary target.

Starter cultures are sold dry in small packets, much like baker's yeast. Once rehydrated, each package is enough to inoculate 400 pounds of meat. For the home producer, always use at least a quarter a packet of starter culture in order to ensure an even distribution of the culture, regardless of how small a batch you are making.

In conjunction with the type of starter culture, the type and quantity of sugar used in the recipe will influence the results of fermentation. The more sugar used, the more lactic acid will be produced, and the lower the final pH of the salami will be. Generally, 0.1 percent dextrose will result in a 0.1 pH drop. If you'd like a more acidic salami, just increase the percentage of dextrose in the recipe.

Dextrose (commonly used in homebrewing, and also called glucose) is the preferred sugar for fermentation, as it is easy for bacteria to metabolize, and produces a rapid and predictable fermentation. Standard table sugar (sucrose) can also be used, but is not as easily metabolized by the bacteria. This results in a slower fermentation and a slower drop in pH.

In addition to the type and quantity of sugar used, the temperature of fermentation will also influence the final flavor of a salami. Fermenting with the cooler temperatures will result will be a more mild and traditional acidification, while fermenting at warm temperatures will result in a higher acidifica-

tion. For precise temperatures, refer to the specific starter culture you will be using.

While this level of knowledge will suffice for the majority of salami producers, there are many starter culture complexities to be explored if you're interested. For instance, if you are determined to make a highly acidic salami (a situation unlikely among most home producers), this requires special attention. A very low pH will inhibit the *Staphylococcus* bacteria, and the enzymes produced by these bacteria are necessary for the reduction of nitrate to nitrite. If you were to use dextrose to drop the pH to below 4.8, the rapid drop would not allow enough time for the production of the nitrate reductase enzyme, and your salami would have a high level of residual nitrate. To solve this problem, use a combination of enough dex-

The Detailed Process

It's helpful to get an overview of the process before tackling the details of making salami. Throughout, cleanliness and keeping the meat at cold temperatures are important to limit unwanted bacterial growth. As you're learning the process, always keep space available in your fridge in case you need to cool the meat down partway through.

The process begins with quality meat, relatively free of any connective tissue. This meat is ground, and mixed with fatback, which is a hard and creamy fat. This mixture is combined with salt, curing salt (not optional, as the inside of a salami is oxygen-free), seasonings, sugar (preferably dextrose), and a purchased starter culture (containing bacteria and yeast). Mix all this together and stuff it into sausage casings. You'll notice at this point that the only difference between salami making and standard sausage making is the need for meat that is relatively free of connective tissue, extra vigilance in cleanliness, the use of curing salt, the use of a starter culture, and the requirement of sugar as a food source for the starter culture.

After the salami mixture is stuffed into sausage casings and tied up, you can inoculate the outside with mold if you wish, and then the salami needs to ferment. Fermentation requires a very humid location, with temperatures above 68°F. The high humidity—above 85 percent (accuracy is not important)—stops the casing from drying too early, and the temperature dictates how fast the bacteria will grow and consume the sugar. This in turn influences flavor, much like the temperature of fermenting

trose to drop the pH to below 5.3, and then sucrose (slow to be metabolized) to achieve the rest of the pH drop. This achieves two things: First, you get a strong initial population of bacteria and enough of an initial pH drop to prevent spoilage; and second, there will be ample time for the *Staphylococcus* bacteria to produce the nitrate reductase enzyme, which will remain at work even when the bacteria are no longer active due to the pH drop.

Fermentation involves a complex ecosystem of microorganisms. Much more information is available concerning this process, and if you are interested in learning more, I recommend contacting Chr. Hansen, the Denmark-based company responsible for all of the available starter and mold cultures. The biology of starter cultures has been studied in great detail; Chr. Hansen will be able to provide you with detailed information outlining the many nuances of each starter culture.

beer changes the flavor. Fermentation will take up to 3 days; you can tell it's been successful if the final pH of the meat is 5.3 or below (a pH of 5.3 is a mild salami—traditional European-style, more acidic salamis will have a final pH of 4.8 or below).

Once fermentation is complete, the salami needs to be moved into a location to dry, with an ideal temperature around 55°F, and a relative humidity of around 75 percent. These numbers differ among manufacturers, and precision is not required. Allow the salami to dry, which will take from 3 weeks to several months. After 30 percent of the weight has been lost, it's time to eat.

SOURCING THE MEAT AND FAT

Salami is made with a combination of lean meat and fat. The proportion of meat to fat is variable, but is usually in the range of 70 to 80 percent lean meat and 20 to 30 percent fat. The best meat for salami comes from the upper shoulder of the pig—the coppa/Boston butt—or from the ham. Both have unique traits, but they're equally suited for salami. Spreadable salami is an exception; its spreadable texture comes thanks to its high soft-fat content combined with a fine grind. It's best made from ground belly and jowl. The lower shoulder (front leg) of the pig is not a good option for any salami, as it is filled with connective tissue. This is better utilized in speck, carnitas, rillettes, or ground for cooked sausage.

When you purchase a butt/shoulder, there may be a nice layer of fat included. If you're looking to save time and money, leave this fat and grind it with the meat. A Boston butt that includes a nice layer of fat will be close to 75 percent lean to 25 percent fat, and may require no additional fatback. If this is your chosen method, you'll need to estimate the percentage of fat included in the shoulder, which doesn't need to be a scientific process and isn't going to ruin your salami if you get it wrong.

Alternatively, you can remove this fat and replace it with fatback. If you have access to high-quality fatback, this more labor-intensive process will result in defined particles of creamy fat, which will give a nice final texture. Compared side by side, salamis produced by the two methods will have a slight difference in appearance, but both can be excellent. Premium commercial producers use both methods.

MEAT PREPARATION

Trim and cube the meat and fat. You first want to trim out any tough connective tissue, as there is no cooking step to soften these tissues, and they'll end up stuck in your teeth when you eat the salami. This is often the most labor-intensive step of salami production. Cube the meat and fat to a size you can feed easily into the grinder. Before grinding, partially freeze the meat and fat; this will give you a clean and defined grind, and help you avoid smearing the fat as it warms. Warm fat will coat the meat chunks, or coat the inside of the sausage casing, which will hold the moisture in the salami and may prevent drying, causing your salami to spoil. If you've made a salami that is extremely slow to dry, this might be a cause.

As you are trimming and cubing the meat, you are exposing more surface area of the meat to the cutting

board, knife, and air, and you will introduce unwanted bacteria—it's unavoidable, but you can minimize the growth of unwanted bacteria by taking a few steps.

The first and most obvious precaution is keeping a clean work space, and using clean knives. A dilute solution of unperfumed bleach works well for this (1 tablespoon bleach to 1 gallon water is the maximum recommended concentration with which rinsing is unnecessary).

Second, as you trim and cube the meat, keep any pieces you aren't actively cutting in the fridge, and once everything is cubed, get the meat back in the fridge as quickly as possible. Always keep in mind the temperature of the meat, as food safety should be your biggest concern when making salami.

Finally, don't ever use pre-ground meat, and don't have the butcher grind the meat for you. A fresh, whole cut of meat from the store is relatively sterile inside, but pre-ground meat will have been exposed to any range of microbes and is unusable for salami. Keep in mind that during fermentation you are intentionally exposing the meat to the ideal conditions for bacterial growth, both good and bad. By purchasing pre-ground meat, of which you know nothing, you are taking on an unacceptable risk.

SALAMI CONSTRUCTION

Once the lean meat and fat are ground, they are mixed with all seasonings and starter culture, and stuffed into casings, as detailed on page 36.

MOLD INOCULATION

As with all dry-cured meats, mold will usually appear on the outside of any drying meat. To control mold

growth, inoculate the outside of all salami that will not be cold-smoked with a purchased mold culture (Bactoferm Mold 600 is the standard). Inoculation should occur before fermentation. To inoculate the outside of a salami, rehydrate the mold culture in distilled water, and either spray it on or dip the salami in the mixture. More detail concerning the role of mold is found on page 41.

FERMENTATION

Avoid direct contact between the salts and starter culture, as a high concentration of salt will kill the bacteria in the starter culture.

Before fermentation begins, record the pH of the salami mixture. To do this, reserve a baseball-sized chunk of the meat mixture, and finely chop up a walnut-sized piece of the test meat with a little distilled water (about equal amounts meat and water). Test the acidity with a pH test strip (available from any sausage supply company) or pH meter. Write it down—this is your pre-fermentation pH reference. Wrap the remaining sample of meat in plastic wrap and place it in the fermentation chamber with the salami. You'll test the pH again after fermentation.

If you've been really strict about keeping the meat cold during the production of the salami, when you place the cold salami in the warm, humid fermentation chamber, you'll get significant condensation on the outside of the sausage casing. This isn't a big deal, but can lead to some slight aesthetic flaws. To avoid this, let the salami warm up to room temperature for a couple/few hours before placing it in the fermentation chamber.

To create the ideal fermenting conditions, you need to create a humid space with a temperature above 68 degrees. This can be done in a variety of ways, but a pan of warm water with a small heat source, placed into a plastic box or cooler is an adequate solution. Some resources recommend fermenting in a gas oven, with the door opened a crack—the pilot light provides adequate warmth, but humidity is a concern—that being said, this method has worked for many people. I recommend the use of an analog slow cooker plugged into a temperature controller or plug-in thermostat (the slow cooker needs to be analog instead of digital so it turns on automatically as the temperature controller switches power to the cooker on and off). Fill the slow cooker with water, and place the slow cooker and salami in a box (I use an empty fridge now, but I started with a plastic storage container with eye hooks screwed into the lid from which I hang the salami). Set the temperature controller, and the heat from the slow-cooker will produce ample humidity while maintaining a precise temperature. Using a hot pad plugged into a temperature controller

placed under a pan of water is another technique.

Up to 3 days later, when the salami is done fermenting, and is ready to be moved from the fermentation chamber to the drying chamber, first check the meat's pH to make sure fermentation was successful. Follow the same routine as above, using the plastic-wrapped test meat; if the pH is at or below 5.3, move the salami into your drying space.

DRYING

Other than temperature and humidity concerns, there are only a couple of small things you need to pay attention to during the drying stage. As the salami dries, keep watch for strange mold. If you inoculated with good mold, you'll quickly see a white layer appear, but even so you'll occasionally get unwanted mold. Just wipe it off with a vinegar-soaked towel.

Finally, check the weight of the salami on a regular basis. There is a window of ideal drying, when the meat isn't too raw looking but also isn't too dry. This is based on personal preference, but between 30 and 40 percent moisture loss is standard.

When you eventually cut into the salami, make note of how long it's been hanging, and look to see if there is a dark ring of meat around the outside circumference. Such a dark ring may be a result of too-fast drying. Consider raising your humidity, or restricting the amount of airflow in the chamber if you see this. If you cold-smoked the salami, you may get a dark ring from the smoking process, which is expected.

Remove the casing before eating. If this is difficult, wrap the salami in a damp towel in a plastic bag overnight; the casing should easily come off.

The Step-by-Step Process

If you're an experienced sausage maker, use your established process for constructing the salami. The only critical difference is keeping the starter culture and salt separate, being extra vigilant about temperature, and poking holes in the casing at the end.

INGREDIENTS NEEDED FOR ANY SALAMI

- Meat and fatback
- Salt
- Dextrose (also known as glucose, this is a type of sugar that can be found at any homebrewing shop)
- Cure #2 (sold under a variety of names; do not use Morton's Sugar Cure)
- Sausage casing
- Starter culture
- Butcher's twine

OPTIONAL INGREDIENTS

- Spices and seasonings (Note: It is recommended that you avoid fresh garlic, which can be a carrier of the spores that cause botulism; use dried garlic as an alternative)
- Mold inoculant

EQUIPMENT

- Meat lug (plastic tub)
- Meat grinder
- Sausage stuffer
- Fermentation chamber
- Drying chamber
- pH strips/pH meter and distilled water
- Thermometer/humidity meter
- Sausage pricker (or a needle)

PREPARATION

1. Choose a recipe, and confirm that you have the necessary components. Several ingredients and some equipment will need to be special-ordered.

2. Prepare the mold inoculant, starter culture, and casings. Follow the instructions from the manufacturer for each of these, and never use less than a quarter a packet of starter culture, regardless of how small the batch is.

3. Prepare your fermentation chamber (see page 113). Make sure the temperature is above 68°F and the relative humidity is very high, ideally above 90 percent.

4. If the meat is frozen, defrost it in the fridge. This can take a couple of days, so plan ahead.

5. Cube the meat, being vigilant about removing all connective tissue. Return to the fridge.

6. Weigh the meat, and using this weight as your guide, determine how much fat you need. Cube the fat. Freeze.

7. Before you grind the meat and fat for the sausages, you want the fat to be frozen, and the meat to be partially frozen (but still grindable). Put the meat and fat in the freezer at the appropriate time to reach this consistency.

8. Using the combined weight of meat and fat, measure out all seasonings, salt, sugar, and curing salt. Keep the salt and curing salt separate from the other seasonings.

CONSTRUCTING THE SAUSAGES

1. Taking precautions to keep everything cold, and being careful not to smear the meat or fat, grind the meat, and then grind the fat. If needed, return them to the fridge or freezer to chill. You do not want the meat and fat to rise above 36°F, so have fridge/freezer space available if needed, and measure the temperature regularly.

2. Combine all ingredients with the ground meat, including the starter culture, but do not add the salt, curing salt, and fat yet (adding the fat last limits the possibility of smearing). Mix well, and then add in the salts and fat. Mix again until the ingredients are uniformly combined and an obvious sticky film has formed on the side of the mixing bowl (this is the protein myosin, which acts as a glue and will hold the whole thing together—without they myosin formation, your salami will be crumbly).

3. If needed, return the mixture to the fridge/freezer to chill during this process, but keep in mind that once the salt is added, the mixture will start to become tougher, which doesn't influence the final quality, but which can make stuffing more difficult. Keeping the meat cold is more important than being quick.

4. Fill the sausage stuffer, then stuff and tie the sausages to your desired length.

5. Reserve any remaining meat (use what's in the stuffer horn), and wrap a baseball of meat in plastic wrap. Before you wrap the meat completely, take a piece out to use to get an initial pH reading. To do this, mix approximately equal parts distilled water and minced meat, and take the pH. Write the starting pH on the tags.

6. Poke holes in the sausage, using a sausage pricker or needle. Sterilize the pricker over a flame before using.

7. Weigh each sausage/string of sausages, and tag them with the weight and starting pH.

ACCLIMATIZATION AND FERMENTATION

1. Let the sausages warm up to room temperature before placing them in the fermentation chamber. This limits condensation forming on a cold sausage in the warm, humid fermentation chamber (optional).

2. Inoculate the sausages with mold—you can spray them or dip them in the mold solution.

3. Place the sausages and baseball sample of meat into the fermentation chamber.

4. Take the pH of the sample each day of fermentation. When the sausages have dropped to at least a pH of 5.3, or your desired final pH, remove them from the fermentation chamber. For food safety reasons, this should happen in less than 3 days.

DRYING

-   If you are going to cold-smoke the salami, do it now—remember that cold-smoking will inhibit mold growth, so you needn't inoculate if this is your plan.

-   Place the salami in the drying chamber (see page 142). At first, check on the drying salami at least once a day, and clean off any unwanted mold with a vinegar-soaked towel. Weigh the salami on occasion.

EATING

-   When the salami is ready to eat, remove the casing and slice. Thin salami will dry quickly, and if you don't eat it in time, it will turn into a hard stick of meat. If you won't be eating it immediately, then, freeze the salami in an airtight bag.

Farmhouse Salami

This is a classic, basic salami recipe, designed to showcase the flavors found in quality meat: a slight sourness from the fermentation, a hint of pepper, and a mild saltiness. This is our "house" salami. It can be stuffed into any size or type of sausage casing, and used as a base for any experimentation (see the notes below). This is a good recipe to learn how fermentation adds to the familiar flavors of pork, salt, and pepper.

INGREDIENTS

Pork (78%)

Fatback (22%)

WEIGHT AS PERCENTAGE OF MEAT/FAT TOTAL WEIGHT

2.6%   Salt

0.25% Cure #2

0.25% White Pepper (toasted and coarsely ground)

0.25% Black Pepper (toasted and coarsely ground)

0.20% Dextrose

Starter culture (B-LC 007 is recommended, but any "traditional" culture is acceptable)

Beef middle casings

Mold inoculant

INSTRUCTIONS

1. Grind the pork and fat through a ⅜-inch grinder plate (or coarser).

2. Rehydrate the starter culture, following the manufacturer's instructions.

3. Combine the pork with the seasonings, dextrose, and starter culture. Mix well and then mix in salt, curing salt, and fat.

4. Continue to mix until a sticky coating forms on the mixing bowl.

5. Stuff into beef middle casings. Tie into 12-inch links.

6. Using a sterilized needle or sausage pricker, prick holes across the entire salami.

7. Measure the initial pH and record it on a tag. Wrap up a sample of meat to test pH later.

8. If you're inoculating with mold, spray or dip the salami into the inoculant.

9. Allow the salami to warm to room temperature (optional).

10. Place the salami and test sample into your fermentation space for up to 3 days at 68 to 75°F, or as recommended for your preferred starter culture. Measure the final pH to confirm successful fermentation (a final pH of 5.3 or below should be reached).

11. Weigh the salami. Write down the weight on a tag or piece of masking tape, and attach this to the salami.

12. Hang the salami in your drying space. The salami will dry for several weeks, depending on its thickness, the humidity, and the air movement.

13. The salami is done when 30 percent of the weight has been lost.

NOTE

This recipe is a great way to showcase quality pork, and is also a great base from which to experiment with different breeds, cuts (ham versus shoulder), grinds, and fats (fatback versus shoulder fat versus belly fat). I also like the simplicity of this recipe when I experiment with different fermentation temperatures, starter cultures, and sugar quantities. If you have access to high-quality fatback, consider grinding it coarsely or even chopping it by hand, giving an irregular, "rustic" texture to the salami.

Fennel Salami

This is the classic Italian fennel salami, with a flavor that will be familiar to many people. If you love fennel, you can increase the quantity used, but be careful: It can quickly overpower the flavor of the salami. This salami is classic for a reason, and it's one of our standards.

INGREDIENTS

78%	Pork
22%	Fatback

WEIGHT AS PERCENTAGE OF MEAT/FAT TOTAL WEIGHT

2.6%	Salt
0.25%	Cure #2
0.25%	White Pepper
0.25%	Black Pepper
0.30%	Fennel Seed
0.20%	Dextrose
2%	Red Wine

Starter culture (B-LC 007 is recommended, but any "traditional" culture is acceptable)

Beef middle casings

Mold inoculant

> ### NOTE
>
> This salami can be made into any size casing, and thin hog casings can be used in order to make a quick-drying version.

INSTRUCTIONS

1. Grind the pork and fat through a ⅜-inch grinder plate (or coarser).

2. Rehydrate the starter culture, following the manufacturer's instructions.

3. Combine the pork with the seasonings, dextrose, and starter culture. Mix well, then mix in the salt, curing salt, and fat.

4. Continue to mix until a sticky coating forms on the mixing bowl.

5. Stuff into beef middle casings. Tie into 12-inch links.

6. Using a sterilized needle or sausage pricker, prick holes across the entire salami.

7. Measure the initial pH and record it on a tag. Wrap up a sample of meat to test pH later.

8. If you're inoculating with mold, spray or dip the salami into the inoculant.

9. Allow the salami to warm to room temperature (optional).

10. Place the salami and test sample into your fermentation space for up to 3 days at 68 to 75°F, or as recommended for your preferred starter culture. Measure the final pH to confirm successful fermentation (a final pH of 5.3 or below should be reached).

11. Weigh the salami. Write down the weight on a tag or piece of masking tape, and attach this to the salami.

12. Hang the salami in your drying space. The salami will dry for several weeks, depending on its thickness, the humidity, and the air movement.

13. The salami is done when 30 percent of the weight has been lost.

Genoa Salami

Genoa salami is the kind you buy sliced at a grocery store deli.
This version has the higher acidity that is common in the United States, and is also finely ground, which is a good option for people who don't like big pieces of fat. This recipe may be made with pork, or pork and beef, but because of the risk of *E. coli* only use beef from a trustworthy source—otherwise just replace the beef with pork.

A special casing called a Genoa sack is available for this style, which is a large casing made of two layers of natural pig and beef casings. The Genoa sack holds a lot of meat—more than 5 pounds—and when stuffed full will give you the look of the salami at the deli. If you'd prefer to have several smaller salamis, or don't have the humidity control necessary to dry big items, just substitute a thinner beef middle casing.

There are many different spice combinations found in Genoa salami, and there is no single authentic recipe—so add and subtract ingredients as you wish.

INGREDIENTS

40% Pork
40% Beef
20% Fatback

WEIGHT AS PERCENTAGE OF MEAT/FAT TOTAL WEIGHT

2.6%   Salt
0.25% Cure #2
0.25% White Pepper
0.30% Fennel Seed
0.30% Dextrose
0.30% Garlic Powder

Starter Culture

INSTRUCTIONS

1. Grind the pork, beef, and fat through a ¼-inch grinder plate.

2. Rehydrate the starter culture, following the manufacturer's instructions.

3. Combine the meat with the seasonings, dextrose, and starter culture. Mix well, then mix in the salt, curing salt, and fat.

4. Continue to mix until a sticky coating forms on the mixing bowl.

5. Stuff into a Genoa sack or beef middle casings.

6. Using a sterilized needle or sausage pricker, prick holes across the entire salami.

7. Measure the initial pH and record it on a tag. Wrap up a sample of meat to test pH later.

8. If you're inoculating with mold, spray or dip the salami into the inoculant.

9. Allow the salami to warm to room temperature (optional).

10. Place the salami and test sample into your fermentation space for up to 3 days at 68 to 75°F, or as recommended for your preferred starter culture. Measure the final pH to confirm successful fermentation (a final pH of 5.3 or below should be reached).

11. Weigh the salami. Write down the weight on a tag or piece of masking tape, and attach this to the salami.

12. Hang the salami in your drying space. The salami will dry for several weeks, depending on its thickness, the humidity, and the air movement.

13. The salami is done when 30 percent of the weight has been lost.

Spicy Red Pepper Salami

(Sopressata-Inspired)

This is a basic spicy salami. Use the best ground chile you can (not chili powder—that's a mix of spices). While Italian red peppers would be traditional, my interest is creating a New World version, so I take this opportunity to experiment with the many interesting North American chile peppers and ground chile available online.

Cold-smoking adds a nice complement to the spiciness of this salami, but the salami is delicious with or without it. If you cold-smoke it, don't worry about inoculating it with mold—the smoke will kill the mold spores.

INGREDIENTS

Pork shoulder (75%)

Fatback (25%)

WEIGHT AS PERCENTAGE OF MEAT/FAT TOTAL WEIGHT

2.6%   Salt

0.25% Cure #2

0.20% Hot Red Pepper Powder

0.30% Black Pepper

0.30% Fennel Seed

0.50% Dextrose

0.20% Red Pepper Flakes

0.20% Garlic Powder

5%   Red Wine

Min. ¼ packet Starter F-LC

INSTRUCTIONS

1. Grind the pork and fat through a ⅜-inch grinder plate (or coarser).

2. Rehydrate the starter culture, following the manufacturer's instructions.

3. Combine the pork with the seasonings, dextrose, and starter culture. Mix well, then mix in the salt, curing salt, and fat.

4. Continue to mix until a sticky coating forms on the mixing bowl.

5. Stuff into beef middle casings. Tie into 12-inch links.

6. Using a sterilized needle or sausage pricker, prick holes across the entire salami.

7. Measure the initial pH and record it on a tag. Wrap up a sample of meat to test pH later.

8. If you're inoculating with mold, spray or dip the salami into the inoculant.

9. Allow the salami to warm to room temperature (optional).

10. Place the salami and test sample into your fermentation space for up to 3 days at 68 to 75°F, or as recommended for your preferred starter culture. Measure the final pH to confirm successful fermentation (a final pH of 5.3 or below should be reached).

11. Weigh the salami. Write down the weight on a tag or piece of masking tape, and attach this to the salami.

12. Hang the salami in your drying space. The salami will dry for several weeks, depending on its thickness, the humidity, and the air movement.

13. The salami is done when 30 percent of the weight has been lost.

'Nduja-Inspired Salami

This is a spicy, spreadable salami, which originates in southern Italy. The spreadability comes from the high fat content, as well as the process of grinding the meat and fat twice through the smallest grinding plate. This salami is relatively unknown domestically but is beginning to see a boost in popularity, thanks to the new crew of small-scale salami producers hard at work across the country.

'Nduja has an intense heat, but it's also remarkably balanced because of its high fat content, which makes the heat bearable and short-lived. Don't be afraid of the large amounts of hot pepper—you'll see the same thing in every published 'nduja recipe. Just trust that it'll be delicious, assuming you use high-quality ground hot chile.

To make a true 'nduja, ground Calabria hot pepper is a requirement, but don't let that hold you back from adapting the recipe to create a domestic version. After all, hot red peppers are a New World food, so it stands to reason that there are domestic red peppers worthy of this recipe. I've been experiment-ing with interesting varieties of New Mexican ground chile, and have had great success—but technically, I can't call it 'nduja.

This recipe requires pure, ground chiles—not the blend of spices with which you'd make a bowl of chili. Do not use generic supermarket chili, chile, or cay-enne. You want pure, ground-up chile peppers.

Because of the high fat content, spreadable salami will not lose the standard 30 percent of weight. It's generally recommended that you don't dry spreadable salami for long (a week or so), and that you either freeze the salami or keep it in the fridge and eat it within a couple of weeks.

INGREDIENTS

Pork (jowl and belly)

WEIGHT AS PERCENTAGE OF MEAT WEIGHT

2.6%   Salt
0.25%   Cure #2
25%   Hot Red Pepper Powder
0.20%   Dextrose

Min. ¼ packet Starter Culture

INSTRUCTIONS

1. Grind the belly and jowl through your smallest grinder plate.

2. Re-chill the ground belly and jowl if necessary, and when they're cold, re-grind them through the smallest grinder plate.

3. Rehydrate the starter culture, following the manufacturer's instructions.

4. Combine the pork with the seasonings, dextrose, and starter culture. Mix well and then mix in the salt, curing salt, and fat.

5. Continue to mix until a sticky coating forms on the mixing bowl.

6. Stuff into hog middles. Tie and truss as necessary.

7. Using a sterilized needle or sausage pricker, prick holes across the entire salami.

NOTE

If your temperatures are correct, you can ferment and smoke at the same time—they do not need to be separate steps. Hog middles are not necessary, and if you have other casings available, don't hesitate to use them. For presentation purposes, I like to transfer the salami into a ramekin or Weck jar before serving.

8. Measure the initial pH and record it on a tag. Wrap up a sample of meat to test pH later.

9. Allow the salami to warm to room temperature (optional).

10. Place the salami and test sample into your fermentation space for up to 3 days at 68 to 75°F, or as recommended for your preferred starter culture. Measure the final pH to confirm successful fermentation (a final pH of 5.3 or below should be reached).

11. Cold-smoke the salami for up to several days.

12. Weigh the salami. Write down the weight on a tag or piece of masking tape, and attach this to the salami.

13. Hang the salami in your drying space. Spreadable salamis are ready to eat after only a few days, but you can dry the salami for longer at your own risk.

14. Do not expect a 30 percent weight loss, as the high fat content will not lose water in the same way that lean meat will.

15. Refrigerate for up to 2 weeks, or freeze.

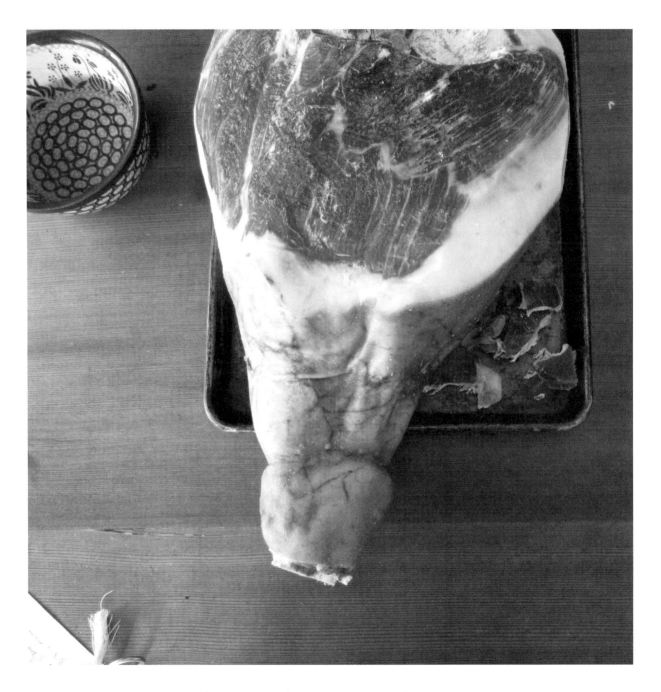

CHAPTER FIVE

Mediterranean Dry-Cured Hams

This section describes the methods for creating a Mediterranean-style dry-cured ham—the ultimate goal for many people interested in dry-curing. These are the hams made famous by Italy's prosciutto di Parma and Spain's jamon serrano and jamon Iberico, but variations are found throughout the Mediterranean region, and there's an ancient dry-cured ham tradition in China as well. These hams are not smoked or cooked, and are characterized by a long drying and aging time and mild salt levels. They're served sliced thin and, as with all dry-curing, eaten raw.

Dry-cured hams are a year-long project, with unique requirements for salting, drying, and aging. While a dry, salty ham is not difficult to make, to perfect the process requires attention to detail and careful control of several variables. With this in mind, I present the process in detail, without simplification.

The science and basic principles of dry-cured hams are no different from those for dry-curing any other whole muscle, but there are several unique vari-ables that require a specialized process. The primary issue relates to the relatively small amount of surface area through which all the salt must be absorbed and through which all moisture must exit. A large ham must absorb a significant amount of salt and lose a significant amount of moisture to be properly dry-cured. Salt and water will not travel through the skin of the ham, so the small area of exposed flesh on the face of the ham is only place for these processes to occur. This fact requires vigilance in preventing the face of the ham from premature drying, which will stop these processes, while also requiring extended periods of cold temperatures in order to stop the ham from spoiling as the salt is slowly absorbed. These criteria require the difficult-to-create environmental conditions of very high humidity, combined with low temperatures—something most home practitioners do not have readily accessible.

Dry-cured hams are big business in Europe, and Europeans have a high standard of quality. The high cost of hanging hundreds of thousands of hams for a year means quality control and standardization are critical in dry-cured ham production. Profitability requires that a minimum of hams be lost to spoilage or inferior quality.

As a result, to the benefit of the home dry-curing enthusiast, European meat scientists have extensively studied dry-cured ham production. Through this research, a step-by-step protocol for the manufacture of premium dry-cured hams has emerged, giving the home producer the benefit of a research-based, standardized process, born from hundreds of years of tradition.

While a precisely detailed process is an invaluable resource for the home curer, the refinement and perfection of the process is in your hands and will depend on your unique variables. Each variation in European dry-cured ham production, from pig breed and diet to variations in time, temperature, humidity, and salt, is the result of countless trials, failures, and successes. In the end, these variations all achieve a similar goal, yet each region's hams have their own unique traits. Use the provided process as a starting point, but adapt it as needed, and don't be discouraged by failure—this is a long, slow journey. I have yet to perfect my dry-cured ham, and it took me nine trials to get a result I was truly happy with, so all I can say is pay attention to everything, be patient, and good luck.

The process I present here is based on data collected, analyzed, and published by a variety of Spanish and Italian meat scientists, and was compiled in Fidel Toldra's 2002 book, *Dry-Cured Meat Products*. If you're interested in more details on Mediterranean ham, I recommend this volume.

Meat

When you purchase a ham, your primary concern should be finding fresh, high-quality meat with the skin on. Short-term freezing does not harm or substantially alter the final product, but will slightly change the rate at which the meat absorbs salt. If you realize you don't have all the components in place for dry-curing a ham, don't hesitate to place it in an airtight bag in the deep freezer for a short period of time.

The best dry-cured hams are traditionally taken from older pigs (18 to 24 months of age), as they have higher fat content, a better flavor profile, and a more intense cured color. Older pigs are difficult to source—it's not cost-effective to raise them that long—so use the biggest, oldest hams you can find.

TRIMMING AND PREPARING THE HAM

There is no single correct way to trim and prepare a ham, and all the meat in a ham will dry-cure beautifully, so if you don't trim your ham exactly as the Italians or Spanish do, it won't necessarily have an adverse effect on your final product. As long as you remove all hidden pockets where bacteria can grow, you can develop your own style of ham trimming, and don't need to be tied down by someone else's tradition.

The primary factors to consider when trimming a ham pertain to the aitchbone, the hoof, the surface of the exposed flesh, and clearing the femoral artery. Each of these factors is directly related to limiting unwanted microbes. Please supplement the following descriptions with the many videos you can find online.

As you trim the ham, keep any ham scraps for salami. Long, thin pieces can be used for coppiette (page 53).

SPANISH VERSUS ITALIAN HAM PREPARATION

Spain and Italy each prepares and trims its hams in a slightly different manner and many variations within these countries exist. The amount of flesh exposed through this trimming primarily affects the meat's salt absorption and drying rates. The differences don't change the final product significantly, and both methods produce excellent results. You have the luxury of not being beholden to any tradition, so trim your ham as you choose.

I recommend spending some time online looking at photos of Spanish and Italian dry-cured hams to get a better visual of different approaches to ham preparation. Choose a style that you can repeat; make sure that you cut the exposed flesh of the ham in a smooth, uniform manner, without any cuts or opened seams that would allow bacteria into the center of the ham.

Hoof

The hoof may be left on or removed; Italy removes the hoof, Spain leaves it on. In the United States, you may not have a choice about the hoof, depending on who is slaughtering the ham: Some processors are required to remove the hoof before the pig enters the processing facility. If you find yourself with a hoof-on ham and want to remove the hoof, cut on the hoof-end of the flexible ankle joint. Be careful not to cut into the leg bone that extends deep into the ham.

Exposing the inside of the bone opens up an easy spoilage pathway to the interior of the ham. It's okay to leave the end nub of bone you removed attached to the leg/ankle joint.

Aitchbone

Removing the aitchbone is optional, with Italy removing it, and Spain not. The aitchbone is simply the hip bone of the pig. The ball of the femur, which is the biggest bone in the ham, sits in the socket of the aitchbone.

If you look at an Italian ham, because the aitchbone has been removed, you'll see the exposed ball of the femur. Most available dry-cured ham tutorials suggest you remove the aitchbone, but this is simply

a reflection of prosciutto di Parma's wide influence, and is not necessarily a superior method. Spanish hams are considered by many to be the best in the world, so clearly aitchbone removal is not the critical variable. Aitchbone removal should be based on your preference, not an assumption that one method is better or more authentic than the other.

If you choose to remove the aitchbone, move slowly, using the tip of the knife to make a series of small smooth cuts against the bone, and focus on extracting a meat-free bone while avoiding any deep cuts into the meat.

To begin the removal, locate what is probably the only exposed bone on the cut face of the ham. This is the aitchbone—or if it isn't, it will lead you to the aitchbone. Keeping the tip of your knife against the hard surface of the bone, gradually work downward, separating meat and bone until you reach the ball/socket junction. Here, slice through any membranous tissue and cut through the small tendon that connects the ball and socket, disconnecting the aitchbone from the femur.

Pull back on the exposed aitchbone. Notice how it's free from the femur, but a branch of the bone still drops deep into the meat. At this point cutting the bone entirely out of the ham isn't difficult, but by exposing this extra surface area of the meat, you're opening up the area to contamination—or at least overdrying—thus decreasing the overall quality of the ham. To avoid this, many Italian producers will saw the aitchbone in half, removing the half that contains the femur socket and leaving the half that

goes deep into the meat. To make this cut, use a bone saw or hacksaw, and cut through the aitchbone as close to the ham's surface as you can without tearing up the meat.

I currently leave the aitchbone in my dry-cured hams, as I like the shape and drying characteristics of a ham with the bone in. I use a difficult-to-describe method for removing the ham, with aitchbone intact, from the carcass without using a bone saw.

Shaping and Smoothing the Ham

Whether or not you remove the aitchbone, the next step of ham preparation is creating a smooth, uniform surface on the exposed flesh, with no pockets where bacteria can grow. Any gaps between the muscle groups, holes from the aitchbone, or other bacterial hiding places need to opened up to allow salt penetration and air circulation. It may seem wasteful to cut away good meat (save it for salami) from a nice ham, but this final trimming needs to be thorough. Use a sharp, clean knife, and shave off layers of meat until the ham has a consistent and smooth face.

Clearing the Femoral Artery

The final step before salting is clearing the femoral artery of any blood that did not drain. Any remaining blood will be prone to spoilage, and the blood needs to be massaged out to block a potential entry point for bacteria.

To clear the artery, picture the ham as a big, almost empty tube of toothpaste; you'll use the palm of your hand to squeeze out the very last bit. Starting on the hoof-end and working toward the cut face of the ham, apply strong pressure with your hand as you slide it toward the ball of the femur, which is near where the femoral artery emerges.

Do this several times on both sides of the leg bone, and you might see a small amount of blood exude from the ham, near the femur ball. Repeat until no more blood remains.

PIG BREED, DIET, AND AGE

The details of pig genetics and diet are beyond the scope of this book, but of the four primary variables described by Fidel Toldra as influencing the quality of the final dry-cured ham, it's important to note that three out of the four variables occur before the animal is slaughtered:

- Genetic types of pigs

- Age at slaughter (5 to 18 months)

- Type of feeding

- Processing technology (type of salting, post-salting duration, processing conditions, drying/ripening/aging conditions, et cetera)

Pig breed and diet also influence flavor, texture, color, and how the ham will absorb salt and dry. Spanish acorn-fed hams are considered the world's best, as the acorns contain an ideal fat profile that results in a well-marbled raw product.

If you're working to perfect your dry-cured ham, one more variable that can affect the final ham is the starting pH of the raw meat. A wide range of pH can result in a good ham, but ideally the starting pH of the ham after it's rested for at least 24 hours after

slaughter should be between 5.6 and 6.2. Disregard this variable until you've figured out the rest of the process.

Salting

The same two general approaches to salting any whole muscle of pork apply to hams as well. The first method, using a precise percentage of salt based on the weight of the ham, is traditionally used by the Italians, and is the method I recommend. The second method, traditionally used by the Spanish, is bulk salting, and requires covering the entire ham with an excessive amount of salt; the final saltiness is controlled by the amount of time the ham is exposed. When you're bulk salting, the rate of salt absorption is connected to several variables and is, as a result, hard to predict for the home producer. For more detail on bulk salting, refer to the Spanish jamon recipe on page 155.

Curing salt is optional in dry-cured ham production: The Spanish use it, the Italians don't. I do use curing salt, most importantly because I'm not willing to expose my family to botulism, no matter how insignificant that risk may be—but also because of the flavor contributions. Carefully consider the conditions your ham will be exposed to before making your decision about curing salts.

SALTING BY WEIGHT

Salting by weight involves measuring a precise salt quantity based on the weight of the ham. The method is traditional in parts of Italy, but is now widespread

in dry-cured ham production. Because of the precise control it gives you over the final salt level, I recommend it for home production.

The process involves packing a measured amount of salt and optional curing salt onto the exposed flesh of the ham, onto the skin, and into the exposed/cut hoof. The salt will only be absorbed through the exposed flesh, but salting the skin and the exposed/cut hoof is important for limiting bacterial growth.

Temperature and humidity are primary variables for the success of this, with high humidity and low temperatures being the goal. The low temperature keeps microbial growth to a minimum as the salt is absorbed, and the high humidity allows for a thin layer of moisture on the outer surface of the ham; the salt dissolves into this moisture, and will then be absorbed into the ham. The high humidity also stops the ham from premature drying, which would prevent the salt from distributing through the meat, creating a too-salty outer layer and an undersalted interior.

You'll apply a total of 3 to 5 percent of the ham's weight in salt to the exposed flesh over a week or so. First apply about two-thirds of the salt, with the thickest application surrounding the femur ball. As the salt is slowly absorbed into the ham, continue adding the reserved salt until you've used it all. The time required for salt absorption varies, but may take up to four weeks.

Watch how the ham absorbs the salt, remembering that the salt will eventually distribute relatively evenly through the ham. Regardless, if you're worried about the process, and it will bring you peace of mind, don't hesitate to add a

little extra to any area that seems too soft, or that absorbed the salt especially quickly—a salty ham is better than a rotten ham.

Use a separate portion of salt to coat the skin of the ham, preventing microbial growth. Various resources suggest a total of 1 to 3 percent of the ham's weight in salt packed onto the skin, but since this salt will not be absorbed into the meat, precise measuring isn't so important. Mix water (approximately 20 percent) with the salt to help it adhere to the skin. You can replenish the salt on the skin as needed.

Lastly, to block bacterial pathways into the center of the ham, pack an unmeasured amount of salt into the cut hoof-end of the leg and, if needed, around the ball of the femur.

After completing the salting process for a couple of hams, you'll start to learn how the meat and salt interact, and you'll begin refining your process. Until then, take notes. If you do add extra salt, I suggest weighing each additional application. When you taste the ham, you'll know the exact percentage of salt you used.

The temperature should be below 40°F (this is the same temperature achieved by salting whole-muscles in the refrigerator). Humidity needs to be high—over 80 percent—for salt absorption, and to prevent premature drying as the salt equilibrates within the ham.

The Schedule

Dry-curing a ham in this style requires three distinct stages:

- Salting (up to 3–4 weeks if salting by weight); below 40°F, 80–90 percent relative humidity

- Post-salting (up to 2 months); below 40°F, 75–90 percent relative humidity, with high humidity being most important in the early stages

- Drying/ripening/aging (6-plus months); 45–75°F, 65–80 percent relative humidity

SALTING

Keep the salted ham below 40°F and above 80 percent humidity for up to 4 weeks—but most likely you'll need much less time than this, depending on the size of your ham, the amount of surface area

> ### SALTING BY WEIGHT
>
> - 3–5 percent salt on the exposed flesh, gradually added as the initial layer of salt is absorbed
> - Example: 12,000g ham × 0.035 = 420g salt
> - 0.25 percent Cure #2
> - Example: 12,000g ham x 0.0025 = 30g Cure #2
> - Approximately 1–3 percent salt on the skin (mixed with approximately 20 percent water to help it adhere)
> - Salt as needed on the exposed cut of the hoof-end

exposed, the physical structure of the meat, and the temperature and humidity of your space.

Place the ham on a rack or cut some lengths of dowel/sticks for the ham to sit on in a container; make sure the ham has air circulation around it, and isn't sitting in any liquid. Regularly remove any exuded liquid from the container—I use a turkey baster for this. Once the salt has all been absorbed, clean off any residual salt and impurities from the salt. The ham will lose about 3 to 4 percent of its original weight during this time.

Note that the conditions of cold temperature and high humidity may be difficult to achieve. Expect some trial and error as you adapt the process to your actual conditions.

POST-SALTING

Immediately after the initial salting, the concen-

tration of salt in the outer layer of the ham is much higher than it is in the ham's interior. The salt now needs time to spread throughout the ham. The salt diffuses slowly. In the biggest hams, the concentration should reach equilibrium within 60 days; less time is needed in smaller hams.

The cool temperature and high humidity of the post-salting stage are important to limit microbial growth as the salt slowly diffuses through the ham. It is during this time that the ham is most prone to spoilage.

The conditions for post-salting are almost identical to the salting stage. Assuming you have your temperature and humidity figured out, the process is relatively hands-off, although you should always check on your ham frequently.

The ham will start to lose moisture during this process, but excess drying will stop the diffusion of salt through the ham, so it's important to maintain a high humidity that limits drying. Commercial producers begin this stage at a high humidity and lower the humidity over the 2 months. By the end of this stage, the ham should have lost an additional 4 to 6 percent of its weight.

DRYING/RIPENING/AGING

This is the time where the ham transitions from a wet, salty piece of raw meat into a dry-cured ham. There are two distinct aspects of this stage, drying and aging (which is also called ripening). Drying refers to the ham losing water, and once the ham has dried adequately, the ham is sealed with a lard mixture and left to age for months/years.

With the salt reaching equilibrium throughout the ham, you can now move the meat to a warmer spot without concern over spoilage. Warm temperatures are important to promote enzyme activity, which will increase the final flavor complexity of the ham, and promote the reduction of nitrate to nitrite.

Drying is arguably the most important variable beyond the quality of the original raw meat, and the majority of moisture lost from the ham happens at the early stage of this process. The key variables influencing drying are temperature, humidity, and air movement in the chamber. Additionally, the amount of flesh exposed when you trim the ham, and the amount of mold growth on the face of the ham, influence the rate at which it loses moisture. It may seem overwhelming now, but eventually you will be considering all these factors when drying and aging your ham.

While there is a certain amount of variation in each region's approach, the drying temperature you use for hams is the same one used for all this book's other recipes; while the humidity is at the high end of normal. Air movement should be minimal and indirect—you want very slow air circulation.

Moisture is not lost through the skin. This gives the ham a relatively small amount of surface area from which moisture can evaporate; even a small amount of premature drying and crust formation can thus have a negative impact on the drying process. Additionally, because a ham is made of many different muscle groups, too-fast drying can cause separa-

tion of these different muscle groups, opening up the inside to spoilage.

To control the drying process, carefully consider the airspeed and humidity within the chamber. Constantly monitor these variables, and fine-tune them as needed. Over time you'll get to know your drying space, and will create a drying regime that fits your conditions.

While I don't have the empirical evidence, I'm convinced it's important that fresh air circulate through the drying chamber on a regular basis. This can be as simple as opening the door every day; or you can set up a timer-controlled exhaust fan to draw in fresh air regularly. Ham enthusiasts have a tendency to pontificate about how the Mediterranean breeze is essential for the best dry-cured hams, and while I tend to be skeptical of such claims, if it is the case, I see no reason to think that a fresh Vermont breeze can't help to create a world-class Vermont dry-cured ham. (I'd attribute the superior quality of Mediterranean hams to the pigs, their diet, and most importantly, the experienced and skilled workforce who care for them.)

Regularly weigh the ham during the drying process. When it has lost 30 percent of its original weight, it's time to seal the ham, preventing more moisture loss while aging and flavor development occur.

As the ham ages, enzymes are slowly breaking down proteins and lipids. The building blocks of proteins and lipids are much more flavorful and aromatic than the proteins and lipids themselves; for more detail, see page 40

SEALING THE HAM

In order to continue aging and flavor development of the ham without overdrying, all exposed flesh needs to be sealed, and the Italians use a mixture they call sugna to do this. Many variations on this mixture exist, with the standard being some combination of rice flour and rendered fat (lard). Kidney fat is recommended, but if you don't have this, don't worry about it. Mix the rice flour (some domestic producers use cornmeal) and fat into a spreadable paste, clean the ham's face of mold, and spread the mixture across all the exposed meat. Peppercorns are occasionally added to the fat, or pressed into it after it's been applied, and are thought to deter pests.

After you seal the ham, it will be relatively stable; it's just a matter of aging for flavor and texture to develop. Temperature and humidity are no longer so critical; as long as you keep the ham at a moderate temperature and humidity, it should be relatively maintenance-free.

Keep the ham hanging until it's at least 9 months old, but ideally leave it for at least a year. The most expensive Spanish hams are aged for three years, so there's no rush.

OTHER NOTES

Pest Control

Some domestic regions that produce country-style hams (an American dry-cured ham, often underappreciated, but with the best examples rivaling European hams) in the southeastern United States wrap the ham in a cloth or bag while curing, drying, and aging. This is to regulate drying speed, but can also act as a barrier to insects and rodents. If you live in a place where such pests might be a concern, make sure you have a plan to limit their access to your ham.

Building a screened-in box to keep out pests is a common solution to this problem.

Accelerating the process

Many ham producers are embracing methods to speed up the process. One method is deboning the ham before salting, which increases the surface area for salt absorption, reduces the distance salt must travel to equilibrate within the ham, and speeds up drying. Faster drying is not always desirable, but assuming overdrying can be prevented by coating the exposed flesh with lard, then aging time can be extended as needed for flavor development. La Quercia of Iowa debones most of their hams before salting begins, and they sell an excellent product.

Microorganisms

BENEFICIAL MICROBES

The primary microbes involved in dry-cured ham production are the same molds, yeasts, and bacteria that will populate the outside layer of any dry-curing.

The primary bacteria involved are a small population of lactic-acid-producing bacteria populating the outside layer of the ham, and *Staphylococcus* bacteria. The latter are found in small populations throughout the meat and supply the nitrate reductase enzyme that will convert nitrate to nitrite.

PATHOGENIC/SPOILAGE MICROBES

Unfortunately, the outer layer of a ham may conceal spoilage bacteria at work deep within, and spoilage will occasionally happen to even the most careful producer. I have aged a ham for a year; it looked per-fectly normal, and until I cut it open I did not realize that the inside was rotten. This experience is enough to kill any enthusiasm for dry-curing, but assuming good technique, this should rarely happen. As I looked over my curing schedule, I realized I hadn't given the ham enough time in cold temperatures for the salt to equilibrate. As I've learned since then, this is the most common cause of spoilage.

If you experience any spoilage or off-odors on the surface of the ham, it may be from accidental cuts and nicks in the face, or from too-slow drying. Be careful in your original ham trimming, and keep a close eye on your drying conditions.

Commercial producers obviously can't take the risk of shipping a spoiled ham, so they've developed methods for identifying flaws in the interior of the hams. Traditionally, the identification of spoiled or sub-par dry-cured hams is done with a probe made of horse bone. The probe is inserted into several points of the ham, and then immediately smelled by a trained expert. I don't have a horse bone probe, and I am unfamiliar with the numerous observations the experts are making concerning the quality of the ham, but having smelled a rotten ham, it's hard to miss, and I would imagine a probe would be a useful way of identifying rot before slicing into a ham. If any readers are in the business of importing horse bone ham probes, please contact me.

Modern technology is changing this process: A mechanical "nose" can be inserted in the ham, and will then analyze volatile compounds to identify defects. This sensor provides precise data on the status of the ham, and removes both human error—but also a skilled worker—from the equation.

Mediterranean-Style Dry-Cured Ham

The Master Recipe

What follows is a dry-cured ham manufacturing schedule modeled after the high-end commercial producers of Spain and Italy. The described method of salting is Italian in origin, but is now widespread, as it is precise and efficient, while the time, temperature, and humidity guidelines given here are an average of those found in several Mediterranean countries.

Expect many of the variables to be unpredictable as you learn the process, and keep in mind that these described conditions are found in purpose-built, modern facilities, using a tightly regulated pork supply, and therefore represent an unrealistic ideal for the home producer. Use this as a starting point, and adapt as needed.

INGREDIENTS

One raw ham, skin on, trimmed, with hoof and aitchbone on or off (see page 135)

Salt

Cure #2

WEIGHT AS PERCENTAGE OF MEAT WEIGHT

3–5% Salt (flesh)

0.25% Cure #2 (flesh)

abt. 3% Salt (skin)

EQUIPMENT

- Plastic bin (big enough to hold the ham, small enough to fit in your fridge)

- Heavy-duty twine

- Scale (up to 30 pounds)

ENVIRONMENTAL CONDITIONS & TIMES

- Salting: Up to 4 weeks. Below 40°F and 90 percent relative humidity.

- Post-salting/resting/salt equilibration: Up to 60 days for a large ham; below 40°F and 75–90 percent relative humidity. (Humidity can be lowered throughout this stage.)

- Drying: 4-plus months (until 32-plus-percent of original weight is lost); 55–60°F, 75% humidity.

- Aging: Seal the meat. Age at 65°F and 65 percent humidity until the ham is at least 1 year old. (Wide variability in these conditions is acceptable)

INSTRUCTIONS

PREPARING YOUR HAM AND CURING SPACE

1. Trim the ham as desired (page 135), being sure to remove all blood from the femoral artery.

2. Once final trimming is finished, weigh the ham and write it down.

3. Calculate the amount of salt and curing salt needed. Write it down.

4. Measure out the salt and curing salt needed for the flesh of the ham.

5. Measure out the salt needed for the skin, and mix this with approximately 20 percent water, creating a damp, packable consistency. The purpose of this salt is simply to limit bacterial growth; it will not be absorbed into the ham. Curing salt is also unnecessary for the skin.

6. Prepare what you will be using to hold the ham. If you're using a plastic bin, consider placing a couple of lengths of wood under the ham, keeping it off the bottom and allowing for airflow around the entire ham.

APPLYING SALT TO THE FLESH, SKIN AND HOOF OF THE HAM

1. Before adding salt, Paul Bertolli says to hit the skin side of the ham with a rolling pin repeatedly to tenderize the ham. I don't argue with Mr. Bertolli, so hit the skin side of the ham with a rolling pin 20 times or so.

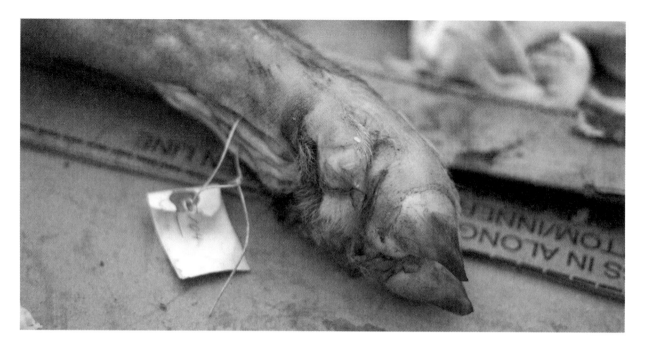

2. Apply the damp salt to the skin side of the ham. Place the ham in the bin, skin-side down.

3. Pack a thick layer of salt onto the exposed flesh. Stop before it starts falling off. Reserve the extra salt (you'll slowly add this as the original salt is absorbed).

4. Pack an unmeasured amount of salt into or around the foot-end of the leg. If the hoof is still attached this is less important, but at least clean out the hoof. Reapply this salt as needed through the process. If the hoof is on, stuff salt into the spot where the tendon is.

5. Move the ham into your salting space. You may want to put a block under one end of the bin; liquid will collect at the other end.

SALT ABSORPTION

Up to 4 weeks.
Temperature below 40°F and 90–95% relative humidity.

1. Frequently drain the bin of exuded liquid. I use a clean turkey baster to remove liquid so I don't have to move the ham and disturb the layer of salt. You can discard this liquid; don't worry about losing any salt that may be in it.

2. As the original layer of salt is absorbed, use the reserved salt to replenish it. Continue this until all the salt has been absorbed.

3. Watch the ham as it absorbs the salt. I've never needed a full 4 weeks for the salt to be absorbed.

POST-SALTING/RESTING

At this point you can hang the ham, but if you've created a high-humidity space that doesn't have space for hanging, that's okay; just make sure the ham is tilted so moisture can drain.

Up to 60 days for a large ham, less for smaller hams. Temperature below 40°F and 80–90 percent relative humidity (dropping over time)

RIPENING/DRYING

Several months (4-plus).
Temperature below 60°F, and 75 percent humidity. Dry until the ham has lost over 32 percent of its original weight.

1. Tightly tie the twine around the ankle of the ham in preparation for hanging. Weigh the ham.

2. Hang the ham in your drying space.

3. Regularly check on your ham and look for any unwanted mold growth. White, flat mold is expected, and can be left, but anything else should be cleaned off with a vinegar-soaked towel.

4. Occasionally weigh the ham to check on its progress.

5. When the ham has lost 32 percent of its original raw weight, it has lost enough moisture for preservation purposes; it's now ready for extended aging. The ham can be eaten now, but aging will improve flavor.

MATURATION/AGING

Up to 3 years.
65°F, 65 percent relative humidity, but variable conditions are acceptable (within reason).

1. Clean the mold off the ham, and clean the surface with vinegar. Let it dry.

2. Seal the flesh of the ham with a rice flour/lard mixture (ideally kidney-fat lard). Making sure not to leave any air pockets, uniformly layer the mixture across all the exposed flesh. The layer does not need to be thick—just enough to seal the ham.

3. There is potential for insect or rodent damage to your ham as it ages. To avoid this, add peppercorns to the lard sealing the ham, wrap the ham in paper bags and/or cheesecloth, or keep it in a screened area.

4. Leave the ham to age until it's at least 1 year from the initial salting.

Alternative Methods

The following methods are variations on the basic dry-cured ham procedure. I haven't edited these methods and procedures in any way; I present them with all the traditional quirks of each region.

Prosciutto di Parma

This prosciutto di Parma recipe and process was outlined by G. Parolari in his 1996 article "Review: Achievements, Needs and Perspectives in Dry-Cured Ham Technology: The Example of Parma Ham" (*Food Science and Technology International* 2[2]).

TRADITIONAL ITALIAN HAM PREPARATION

- Hoof off.

- Skin on.

- Aitchbone partially removed: Remove the aitchbone socket from the femur ball, and then cut the aitchbone where it plunges into the meat. The bone may need secondary trimming after the ham has dried, and before the ham is sealed.

SALTING QUANTITIES, FIRST ADDITION

- Add salt totaling 2–3 percent of the ham's weight to the exposed flesh.

- The skin should be coated in approximately 1–2 percent salt (make a 4:1 salt/water mixture to help the salt adhere to the skin).

- Place an unmeasured amount of salt in the cut foot-end.

- No curing salt is used in authentic prosciutto di Parma production.

SALTING QUANTITIES, SECOND ADDITION (AFTER 1 WEEK)

- On the flesh, add 1 percent less salt than you used in the first addition.

- Add extra salt on the skin, the cut leg, and a little around the ball of the femur.

SALTING

- First salting: 1 week at 34–40°F, humidity 75–90 percent.

- Second salting: 3 weeks at 34–40°F, humidity 70–80 percent.

POST-SALTING/RESTING (REPOSE)

- First resting stage: Hang the ham for 2 weeks below 40°F at 50–60 percent humidity.

- Second resting stage: Hang the ham for 6 weeks below 40°F at 70–80 percent humidity.

RIPENING/DRYING

- 4-plus months at 55–60°F, 75 percent humidity (until 32–36 percent total moisture is lost).

AGING/MATURING

- Wash off the remaining salt, mold, et cetera, let the ham dry, and seal it with a rice flour/fat mixture. Age at least until the ham is 1 year old.

- Age up to 3 years at 65°F, 65 percent humidity.

Spanish Jamon Variation

This method is primarily found in Spanish jamon production, but also in parts of Italy and France. After salting has finished, follow the master dry-cured ham recipe.

In Spain, hams are grouped by similar size, rubbed with a pre-salt layer of Cure #2, and stacked in large bins, which are then filled with salt.

This method is difficult to refine for home production, because so many variables influence the rate of salt intake by the ham. If you're intent on using this method, consider the amount of skin removed from the ham and the amount of flesh and fat exposed; salt intake will differ across each of these surfaces. Standardize your method for trimming the ham, so you can focus on the other variables and eventually adjust the amount time for salt absorption per kilogram.

Salt absorption is also influenced by pH, water content, and structure of the muscle. For especially wet hams, or hams that have been frozen and thawed, the time may be reduced by up to 2 days. For especially large hams, you can remove the meat from the salt partway through the process, wash it, and put it back under the salt.

The addition of nitrite and nitrate is done before the hams are placed under salt, traditionally by hand or by tumbling the ham with the nitrate. For the inexperienced home producer, these methods will result in a wide variation of nitrate and nitrite levels in your final product.

BULK SALTING (JAMON)

- Typical Spanish hams are salted for 1.1 days per kilogram.

- The temperature should be below 40°F.

- Humidity should not drop below 75 percent.

- Rub the ham with Cure #2. Precise quantities of curing salt will be difficult to calculate when bulk salting—the longer the ham is in the salt, the more nitrite and nitrate will be absorbed.

The schedule for salting, post-salting, and aging is the same as any other ham, except the time for salt absorption will be adjusted as described above.

CHAPTER SIX

Enjoying Your Dry-Cured Meat

After months of careful tending to your drying meat, you are finally ready to enjoy the fruits of your labor. If you turn out to be anything like my family, you will eat the majority of your meat fresh off the slicer or cutting board, without additional preparation or ingredients, except maybe some fresh squeezed lemon and cracked pepper.

Once you've eaten your fill of simple, sliced meat, consider which of your favorite breakfast, lunch, or dinner recipes might benefit from the addition of dry-cured meat—either sliced or crisped in a pan or under a broiler. You shouldn't need recipes to use your dry-cured meat, as it makes everything taste better. Still, I've included a few of our go-to uses. Keep in mind that when dry-cured meat is warm, it will taste much saltier than when it's cold. Adjust the salt levels of your standard recipes appropriately.

In this chapter, you will find a few ways we showcase our favorite products. Some of the specific details pertaining to ingredients or amounts have intentionally been left out in order to highlight the idea that these suggestions are flexible and forgiving. So go get your first cut and start creating.

Slicing, Serving, and Storing Your Meat

If you wish to fully appreciate your dry-cured meat, the meat must be sliced thinly (pancetta and guanciale are exceptions since they're usually cooked—slice these like bacon). A thin slice will always provide a better flavor, texture, and overall experience than a thick slice of dry-cured meat, which will be tough and salty, regardless of the quality. Slicing dry-cured meats thinly is difficult; master Spanish jamon slicers spend years perfecting the art. Fortunately, for the rest of us, with a little practice, or by using a meat slicer, paper-thin slices of meat are obtainable.

The trick to slicing any dry-cured meat, whether it's a ham, coppa, or salami, is not trying to get a full, complete slice every time. It's more important to slice a small piece of the meat thinly than to get a whole cross section of it. Watch the Spanish jamon slicers, and you'll notice they only cut slices the size of a credit card or smaller. We're used to seeing big, complete slices of deli meat taken from a meat slicer, but when slicing by hand, small slices are ideal.

Slicing by hand is a slow process, and while there is a certain satisfaction to it, after working your way through a coppa or two, you'll come to the logical conclusion that life would be better with a meat slicer. Good decision. Meat slicers are dangerous, and require your complete and sober attention, but they will provide you with a constant supply of perfect slices.

SLICING A HAM

Slicing a ham is a different process than slicing any other dry-cured meat. Hams can be deboned and placed on a slicer, but for the most impressive presentation a ham stand is necessary. In our house it is a Christmas tradition for a dry-cured ham to be sitting in a stand on the kitchen counter, tempting anyone who walks by to cut a few slices. Ham stands are available from many different online sources, and I'm going to assume that if you're willing to take a year to make a dry-cured ham, you'll also go watch some videos depicting proper ham-slicing technique. This is another case where a video will make everything easier, and there are many well-made how-to slicing videos available.

PACKAGING AND STORING WHOLE CUTS OF DRY-CURED MEAT

Do not leave your half-eaten dry-cured meats in the fridge for long periods of time. They will not spoil, but the quality will quickly deteriorate. Ideally, store any dry-cured meats that you are not eating in a vacuum-sealed bag in a deep freezer. If you do not have a vacuum sealer, you can tightly wrap the meat in plastic wrap, place it into a freezer bag, and freeze. Whatever your method, the goal is to keep the meat in an airtight, frozen condition, which will allow you to keep it in the freezer for a long period of time.

PACKAGING AND STORING SLICED MEAT

A vacuum sealer will allow you to store and transport already sliced meat without a significant loss in quality. Lay the slices flat on a piece of parchment paper; for the most professional appearance, overlap the slices so they are all facing the same direction, with the meat and the fat of each slice lining up. Vacuum-seal the meat on the parchment paper and freeze. If this package will ever be kept at room temperature, curing salts should be used due to the oxygen-free environment.

Suggestions for Eating Your Dry-Cured Meats

I've included some full recipes, but here are a few easy ideas to get you started.

SLICED AND PLATED

One of the most satisfying parts of dry-curing is making a beautiful plate of thinly sliced meat. Try drizzling olive oil, lemon juice, and cracked pepper over coppa, or serving rolls of prosciutto with fresh figs or cantaloupe. This is a great appetizer to carry to any party, and it can make a birthday brunch extra special.

BREAKFAST SANDWICH

Thanks to a continuous supply of farm-fresh eggs from my parents, we are big egg eaters. This is great, because eggs and salty pork go very well together. Try layering an English muffin with a fried egg, any Alpine-style cheese, avocado, and crisped spicy coppa. Good coffee and hot sauce should accompany this meal.

SAVORY SCONES OR BISCUITS

Add crisped and roughly chopped prosciutto and sharp Vermont cheddar to your favorite scone or biscuit recipe. Eat with butter and some homemade jam or jelly. Again, add a good cup of coffee and you can rival any trendy breakfast joint.

THE FARM SANDWICH

One of my family's summertime traditions is to spread a lunch table with cutting boards of salami, Monterey Jack cheese, fresh tomato, red torpedo onion, avocado, and a loaf of sourdough bread. Any salami will work, but try fennel, farmhouse, and sopressata to explore a range of flavor profiles.

Vermont Farm Salad

Makes: 2-4 servings

The acidity of this salad recipe's delicious vinaigrette complements the saltiness of its cured meat. Both the dressing and the crispy meat are flavorful and will enhance almost anything you want to add. This is a forgiving recipe; for vegetable amounts, you can use whatever you have on hand and adjust for the number of people you're serving.

INGREDIENTS

FOR THE SALAD

8 oz. thinly sliced dry-cured meat (figure 2-3 slices per person)

4-6 handfuls mixed greens

1 Endive, leaves separated

1 Avocado, peeled, pitted and sliced

¼ cup Salted Pistachios

2 oz. Blue Cheese, crumbled

Optional: chopped beets, arugula, tomatoes (if in season), hard-boiled egg

FOR THE DRESSING

¼ cup Vinegar (I like a combination of two vinegars, usually cider and red wine)

2 teaspoons Mustard (use what you have; I like a French Dijon mustard)

Pinch of Salt

Cracked Pepper

¾ cup Olive Oil

Optional: Tarragon, Garlic, Shallot, Lemon

INSTRUCTIONS

1. Preheat broiler. Lightly grease baking sheet.

2. Prepare the meat by laying the slices flat on a baking sheet and placing them under the broiler until they're crispy, but not burned. Remove the pan from the oven and set aside to cool.

3. Meanwhile, make the dressing: Whisk together the vinegar, mustard, salt, and pepper. Slowly add in the oil while continuously mixing. This will make enough dressing for several salads.

4. Once meat is cool, chop it coarsely.

5. Layer the lettuce, vegetables, pistachios, cheese, and chopped meat, add an appropriate amount of salad dressing, and toss well.

Wrapped Figs with Goat Cheese

Makes: 12 appetizer servings

This is a simple recipe and can be modified by substituting any fresh fruit, but figs are my favorite.

INGREDIENTS

12 Figs

8 oz Goat Cheese

Sliced dry-cured meat (prosciutto is ideal, but any other thinly sliced meat will work)

Balsamic Vinegar

INSTRUCTIONS

1. Preheat oven to 400°F. and line a baking sheet with parchment paper or lightly grease pan. Or, prepare grill by lightly greasing rack and starting the fire.

2. Trim stem from figs, and slice in half. Place a teaspoon of goat cheese on the cut side of each fig half, then tightly wrap fig and cheese with a slice of meat.

3. Place the figs onto a baking sheet and place on top rack in oven. Cook until the meat starts to crisp and the goat cheese is warm and soft, about 8 to 10 minutes. Alternatively, you can carefully cook these on a hot grill for about 5 minutes.

4. Drizzle your favorite balsamic vinegar lightly over the figs once they come out of the oven.

Substitutions: Wrap the prosciutto around slices of pineapple, peach, or cantaloupe. I'd recommend omitting the goat cheese for these fruits.

Broad Brook Scones

The addition of salty dry-cured meat complements a buttery scone. Add your favorite jam or jelly and you will have an impressive breakfast. Any crisped dry-cured meat can be substituted for the bacon in this recipe, but whatever you use, dice it into small pieces after you've cooked it for the best flavor and texture. This recipe comes from Greg Russ, whose "Scone Sundays" are always a highly-anticipated event.

INGREDIENTS

1 cup all-purpose flour, plus more for rolling

1 cup whole wheat pastry flour

½ cup sugar

½ teaspoon salt

¼ teaspoon baking soda

2 teaspoons baking powder

½ cup (1 stick) unsalted butter

½ cup milk

½ cup Greek yogurt

2 tablespoons maple syrup

1 cup frozen wild blueberries

¼ pound bacon (weighed before cooking), cooked and finely chopped

INSTRUCTIONS

1. In a large bowl, mix together the flour, whole wheat pastry flour, sugar, salt, baking soda, and baking powder.

2. Cut in the butter.

3. In a separate small bowl, mix together the milk and Greek yogurt. Add this wet mixture to the flour-and-butter mixture.

4. On a floured surface, form the dough into a square, folding it over several times.

5. Put the dough in the freezer for about 5 minutes. Preheat the oven to 425°F and line a baking sheet with parchment paper. Set aside.

6. Remove dough from freezer. On the same floured surface (use more flour if necessary but not too much), roll out the dough into a 12-inch square. Spread the maple syrup over the dough. Sprinkle on the wild blueberries, then the bacon pieces.

7. Roll the dough into a log and use your hands to pat it and shape it into a rectangle that's roughly 12×6. Cut that into four squares, and cut each one of those diagonally so you hae 8 scones.

8. Place the scones on the prepared sheet and place in oven. Bake for 20 to 25 minutes.

Roasted Brussels Sprouts with Pancetta

Makes: 4 servings

Far superior to any boiled brussels sprouts, this is our favorite way to prepare brussels sprouts, which are a staple green vegetable for our family throughout the winter. The recipe results in nicely browned and roasted sprouts, with tender interiors. Add a little crispy, salty pork into the pan at the end, and you'll convert any non-brussels-believers.

INGREDIENTS

1 pound brussels sprouts

2–3 slices Pancetta, cut into ¼-inch matchsticks (lardons)

4 cloves Garlic

1 tablespoon Red Pepper Flakes

Salt and Pepper to taste

INSTRUCTIONS

1. Preheat your oven to 400°F. Trim the brussels sprouts and slice them lengthwise. Set aside.

2. Heat a cast-iron skillet (or any ovenproof pan) over medium-low heat on stove, and cook the lardons until crispy but not burned, 5 to 10 minutes. Remove the meat to a serving dish large enough for the Brussels sprouts, leaving the rendered fat in the pan. (You'll be roasting the sprouts in the pan, so you can drain some of the fat if desired, but leave a thick coating.)

3. Turn the heat up to high, and, once the fat is hot, add the brussels sprouts cut-side down. Add the garlic to the pan along with the red pepper flakes. Allow the sprouts to become browned and caramelized on the cut sides, stirring occasionally, about 5 or 6 minutes. Once they're browned, transfer the pan to the oven. The sprouts will begin to wilt and darken, and any stray leaves should start crisping.

4. After 20 minutes, start checking the brussels sprouts for tenderness. Cook them until they're very tender inside, about 30 minutes. Remove the pan from the oven, and carefully transfer the sprouts to the bowl with the cooked pancetta and gently toss.

5. Taste for saltiness, add some salt and cracked pepper, and stir in some more red pepper flakes if desired.

Speck and Caramelized Onion Pizza

Makes: 2 pizzas

The smokiness of speck goes well on a pizza with the sweetness of caramelized onion. If you don't have speck, use any other thinly sliced dry-cured meat. I haven't provided a recipe for pizza dough here, but if you make your own, make it a few days in advance and store it in pizza-sized dough balls in a leftovers container—the extra time in the cold fridge will improve the flavor and texture of your pizza.

INGREDIENTS

Enough dough for 2 pizzas

1–2 large Sweet Onions

Oil, as needed

Salt to taste

1–2 tablespoons Butter (optional)

1 (28-ounce) can high-quality whole Tomatoes, drained in a colander

Flour, as needed

1 pound whole-milk Mozzarella

Pile of thinly sliced Speck

Pepper to taste

1 tablespoon Red Pepper Flakes

INSTRUCTIONS

1. If your dough is refrigerated, pull it out of the fridge to warm. Heat your oven and pizza stone (if you have one) as hot as possible.

2. Caramelize the onions: Slice the onions thinly and add to a medium-hot pan with enough oil to coat the bottom. Add a generous pinch of salt to the onions, turn the heat down so there is no risk of burning, and cook, covered, until the onions are very soft. Remove the lid and continue to slowly cook the onions until they're darkly caramelized and sweet. Don't hesitate to add a tablespoon or two of butter as the onions are cooking. This whole process may take 45 minutes to reach perfection; the final result should resemble an onion jam.

3. Roughly crush the drained tomatoes with your hands, taking care to remove any stems or skin.

4. Make sure you have all the toppings ready to go and a hot oven. Work quickly once you start shaping the dough to avoid sticking. On a heavily floured surface, press the dough into a pizza-sized circle, flouring underneath as needed to avoid sticking. Transfer the flattened dough to a heavily floured pizza peel, or use a flipped-upside-down cookie sheet covered in flour. If you don't have a pizza stone, you can cook the pizza on a cookie sheet.

5. Add six to eight small piles (2 tablespoons or so each) of crushed tomatoes across the dough. Less is better, and by not creating an even coating of sauce, you'll get more contrasting flavor.

6. Break the mozzarella up with your hands into chunks and place these across the pizza, adding at most 8 ounces per pizza (but less is often better).

7. Add a generous amount of speck to the pizza. The speck will shrink as it cooks, so use more than you think is necessary.

8. Spread the caramelized onions across the pizza in small piles.

9. Crack some pepper across the top, and add red pepper flakes. Slide the pizza into the oven and cook for 10 minutes or so (different ovens will vary widely in cooking times, so watch carefully—but open the oven as infrequently as possible).

10. Carefully remove from oven and let pizza settle for a few minutes. Slice and enjoy.

Pasta Carbonara

We originally obtained this recipe from Salumi Artisan Cured Meats in Seattle, and have been modifying it over the years. The result is a simple and excellent version of the classic dish. This recipe calls for guanciale, but pancetta, or even bacon, will substitute well.

INGREDIENTS

1 pound Spaghetti or Fettuccine

2 tablespoons Butter

¼ pound Guanciale, cut into ¼-inch matchsticks (lardons)

1½ teaspoons Red Pepper Flakes

3 Eggs

2 cups grated Parmesan, Pecorino, or a mixture of the two, divided

Black Pepper to taste

INSTRUCTIONS

1. Cook the pasta in a generous amount of salted water.

2. Meanwhile, brown the butter, and set it aside to cool for a few minutes (you want it to be hot enough to melt the cheese, but not to scramble the eggs). Meanwhile, cook the guanciale with the red pepper flakes. Drain any excessive grease from the guanciale, but don't hesitate to leave a little for flavor.

3. Mix the eggs and 1 cup of the cheese together, and add to the browned butter, stirring rapidly to avoid scrambling the eggs while creating a creamy sauce.

4. Combine the cooked pasta with the egg-cheese mixture, then add the guanciale and pepper flakes, and the remaining cheese. Grind some black pepper and mix well until all the cheese is incorporated.

Glossary

Amino acids

The building blocks of peptides, and therefore the building blocks of proteins. Many amino acids are flavorful and aromatic once they are released from the structure of a protein.

Bactoferm Mold 600

The industry-standard culture for inoculating the outside of drying meat with mold. This culture produces a harmless white mold, which will outcompete most unwanted molds while regulating the drying process and influencing flavor. This is sold in a long-lasting dry form, and is easily rehydrated before use.

Cure #1

A salt mixture used for curing. Also known as pink salt, Cure #1 contains salt (NaCl) and sodium nitrite (NaNO2). This is the industry-standard mixture for curing items that will not be aged for long periods of time. Cure #1 may be referred to by a variety of other names, most containing #1 in the title.

Cure #2

A salt mixture used for curing. Contains salt (NaCl), sodium nitrite (NaNO2), and sodium nitrate (NaNO3). Cure #2 is used when the meat will be aging or resting for more than a couple of weeks, because the nitrate provides a steady supply of nitrite as it breaks down. Cure #2 may be referred to by a variety of names, most containing #2 in the title.

Cure accelerator

See sodium erythorbate.

Curing salt

A generic term for a mixture of salt, sodium nitrite, and sometimes sodium nitrate.

Dextrose

A simple type of sugar that is especially easy for bacteria to process, assuring a quick fermentation. Dextrose is available from any homebrewing store.

Enzymes

Molecules produced by living cells that facilitate many of the chemical reactions necessary to sustain life. Enzymes are non-living. In dry-curing, among other things, they are responsible for breaking down the components of a piece of meat, creating more flavors and better texture. They are also responsible for reducing nitrate to nitrite.

Microbes

Any very small organisms (bacteria, yeast, et cetera).

Mold inhibitor

See potassium sorbate.

Nitrates

Often confused with nitrites, nitrates serve as a long-term supply of nitrites. Nitrates alone do not cure meat, but over time will break down into nitrites, which are very reactive when mixed with meat. Nitrates are used in very small quantities; they are toxic in large doses.

Nitrites

A commonly occurring chemical that reacts with meat to form the traditional flavors and colors of cured meats, while also preventing the growth of the bacteria responsible for botulism. Nitrite was originally sourced from natural mineral deposits, and has been used in conjunction with meat for centuries, if not longer. Nitrites are used in very small quantities; they are toxic in large doses.

Nitrosamines

Formed when nitrites are exposed to very high heat in the presence of compounds called amines. Nitrosamines are potentially carcinogenic, and are the original source of the concern surrounding nitrites. The easiest way to limit nitrosamines in your diet is simply not to burn your food (especially bacon).

Peptides

The building blocks of proteins, made of chains of amino acids.

Potassium sorbate

A common mold inhibitor and preservative. A mold inhibitor will prevent mold from growing on drying meat.

Sodium erythorbate

Commonly called a curing accelerator, sodium erythorbate increases the rate at which nitrite breaks down into its components, which assures that very little residual nitrite remains in the meat. Curing accelerators are harmless, but are unnecessary and unwanted in items that will be dried, aged, or cured for any extended period of time, as eventually the nitrite will naturally break down. Curing accelerators are used in the commercial production of bacon.

Staphylococcus bacteria

A group (genus) of bacteria, mostly harmless, which are commonly found worldwide. Staphylococcus naturally populate drying meat, or can be added through a starter culture when you make any fermented sausage. They are important for producing the enzyme that reduces nitrate to nitrite. Staphylococcus bacteria are inhibited by a low pH.

Starter culture

A mix of bacteria (and sometimes yeast) necessary for producing a fermented sausage (salami). There are many different starter cultures available for purchase, each with its own characteristics. Starter cultures resemble baker's yeast (which is not a substitute), and will last a year refrigerated.

Resources

Portland Meat Collective

Portland, OR

pdxmeat.com

Few people are doing as much to revive the art of home butchering as Camas Davis at the Portland Meat Collective. Take a weekend vacation to Portland and learn from the experts how to break down a pig for dry-curing. You'll learn more about butchering in a 4-hour class than you would from a year of practicing at home.

Underground Food Collective

Madison, WI

undergroundfoodcollective.org

While commercially producing dry-cured meats, operating a restaurant and butcher shop, catering, and offering classes for the public, the Underground Food Collective has also just released the first public-domain version of a Not Cooked Shelf Stable HACCP plan. Critical for anyone interested in commercially producing dry-cured meat, the HACCP plan is a prohibitively expensive food safety plan, required by the federal government, and is the hurdle that stops most people interested in selling dry-cured meats to the public. By releasing this plan in the public domain, the collective has opened up many possibilities for small-scale producers. Support this group of hard workers in any way you can.

Chop Butchery & Charcuterie

Portland, OR

chopbutchery.com

Chop Butchery is a premium butcher that also produces high-quality salami and other dry-cured meats. The folks here have always been willing to answer my butchering and dry-curing questions, and they also make one of the best sandwiches in Portland. Stop in next time you're in the neighborhood.

Butcher & Packer Supply Company

butcher-packer.com

The place for all your dry-curing needs (and everything else meat-related you might want).

The Sausage Maker

www.sausagemaker.com

Another useful website for sausage and salami supplies.

curedmeats.blogspot.com

This site has a substantial amount of information on the step-by-step process of dry-curing pork, along with recipes and links to helpful videos.

sausagedebauchery.com

A source for authentic Italian ingredients and hard-to-find casings, such as beef bladders. The blog that accompanies the site is full of useful information, especially concerning culatello, 'nduja, and speck.

meatsandsausages.com

In-depth technical explanations of everything related to cured meats, dry-cured meats, smoking, sausages, and so on. This is an excellent source of authentic recipes from around the globe.

lpoli.50webs.com

A lifetime's worth of recipes for all types of dry-cured meats, cured meats, and fresh sausages. This is an excellent place to get ideas for your next project.

www.sossai.net/salumi/forum/default.asp

An Italian-language forum concerning cured meats. With a little deciphering of Google Translate's attempt at technical terminology, this is a trove of useful information.

Processing Inspectors' Calculations Handbook

www.fsis.usda.gov/OPPDE/rdad/FSIS Directives/7620-3.pdf
All of the USDA's recommended levels for nitrates, nitrites, curing accelerators, et cetera. Only dive into this if you're interested in fine-tuning levels of these ingredients, and beware that their use of the term dry-cure usually refers to a dry rub, not dry-cured meats.

Zanna Printed Textiles

zannaprintedtextiles.com
The beautiful silk-screened aprons found in this book are made by our friend Zanna Scott in Portland, Oregon.

References

Chizzolini, R., P. Rosa, and E. Novelli. "Biochemical and Microbiological Events of Parma Ham Production Technology." *Microbiologia*, 1993.

Chr. Hansen. *Bactoferm Meat Manual Vol. 1: Fermented Sausages with Chr. Hansen Starter Cultures,* 2nd ed. Hørsholm, Denmark: Author, n.d.

Graham, P., N. G. Marriott, and R. F. Kelly. *Dry-Curing Virginia Style Ham.* Virginia Cooperative Extension Publication 458-223, 2011. http://pubs.ext.vt.edu/458/458-223/458-223_pdf.pdf

Marriott, N. G., and P. P. Graham. *Some Solutions to Difficulties of Home-Curing Pork.* Virginia Cooperative Extension Food Science and Technology Publication 458-872, 2000. http://nchfp.uga.edu/how/cure_smoke/curing_pork.pdf

Ockerman, H. W., L. Basu, F. Leon Crespo, and F. J. Cespedes Sanches. *Comparison of European and American Systems of Production and Consumption of Dry-Cured Hams.* National Pork Board and American Meat Science Association, 2002. http://www.pork.org/filelibrary/factsheets/porkscience/q-drycured%20hams04661.pdf

Parolari, G. "Review: Achievements, Needs and Perspectives in Dry-Cured Ham Technology: The Example of Parma Ham." *Food Science and Technology International* 20, no. 6 (1996).

Rentfrow, G., R. Chaplin, and S. P. Suman. "Technology of Dry-Cured Ham Production: Science Enhancing Art." *Animal Frontiers* 2, no. 4 (October 2012).

Sindelar, J., and A. Milkowski. "Sodium Nitrite in Processed Meat and Poultry Meats: A Review of Curing and Examining the Risk/Benefit of Its Use." *American Meat Science Association White Paper Series* 3 (November 2011).

Toldra, F. *Dry-Cured Meat Products.* Trumbull, CT: Food & Nutrition Press, 2002.

———, ed. *Handbook of Meat Processing.* Ames, IA: Wiley Blackwell, 2010.

USDA Food Safety and Inspection Service. *Generic HACCP Model for Not Heat Treated, Shelf Stable Meat and Poultry Products.* September 1999. http://www.fsis.usda.gov/wps/wcm/connect/0dfb5810-3c95-4470-9fbd-2ba4fcc99344/HACCP-15.pdf?MOD=AJPERES

———. *Processing Inspectors' Calculations Handbook.* 1995. http://www.fsis.usda.gov/OPPDE/rdad/FSISDirectives/7620-3.pdf

ACKNOWLEDGMENTS

Thank you to our brothers, Buck Sleeper and Haskell Kent, for their photography skills, which are on display throughout this book. We sincerely appreciate the time and energy you spent with us on this endeavor.

Lots of love and many thanks to our 4 friends, for all the help and support you have provided, especially over the last two years. We are grateful beyond words. Harlo is a lucky kid.

Thank you to STK for raising the fine pigs found on the pages of this book.

Thank you to Fina, for your watercolor depictions of Sicily. Thank you for being an inspiration to the three of us.

Thank you to Ben Wolfe for sharing your knowledge of mold, to Camas Davis for your teaching skills and recipe help.

Thank you to Ann and everyone else at Countryman Press who patiently guided me through this process.

Most importantly, thank you to DeVeau for being a willing partner from the beginning.

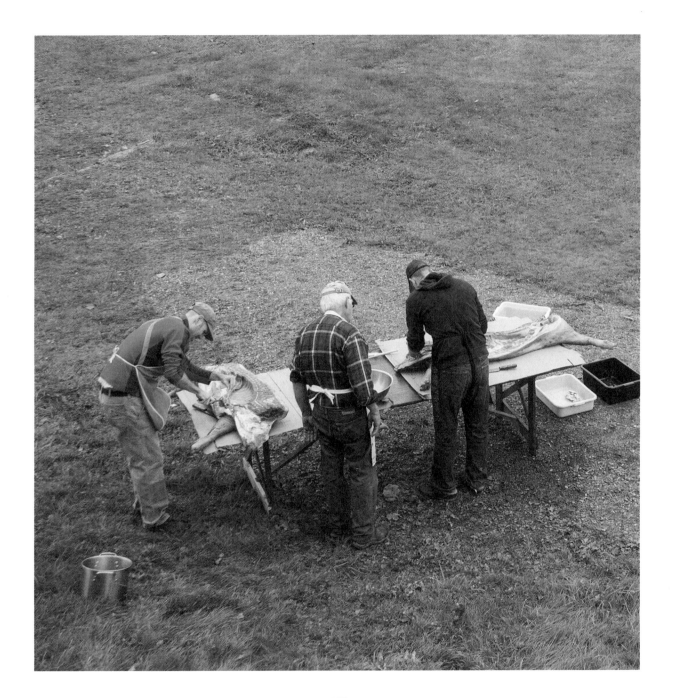

INDEX